THE ORIGIN OF WRITING

The Origin of Writing

Roy Harris

Professor of General Linguistics
in the University of Oxford

Open Court

La Salle, Illinois

OPEN COURT and the above logo are registered in
the U.S. Patent and Trademark Office.

Published by arrangement with Gerald Duckworth & Co. Ltd., London.

© 1986 by Roy Harris

OC 907   10 9 8 7 6 5 4 3 2 1
ISBN: 0-8126-9035-4

Library of Congress Cataloging-in-Publication Data

Harris, Roy, 1931–
   The origin of writing.

   Bibliography: p.
   Includes index.
   1. Writing—History. 2. Alphabet—History. I. Title.
   P211.H35   1985   411   86-2439
   ISBN 0-8126-9035-4

Contents

Preface

'The practice of writing,' says one eighteenth-century authority, 'is of such remote antiquity, that neither sacred nor profane writers give any satisfactory account of its origin.'[1] These words are no less apposite today than they were two hundred years ago. That is hardly surprising, for the intervening centuries have seen remarkably little change in the notion of what a 'satisfactory account' would require, or what stands in the way of giving one.

The difficulty is in part due to a failure to deal squarely with the apparently prior question: 'What is writing?' Perhaps that is because 'What is writing?' sounds like a simpleton's question, to which perfectly straightforward answers are readily available. There is, indeed, a sense in which everyone in a literate community already knows what writing is. But that sense, unfortunately, yields only a circular definition: writing is what we learn to do when we are taught to write. Perhaps, on the other hand, 'What is writing?' sounds like a Socratic question (cf. 'What is virtue?'); and the trouble with Socratic questions, as everyone knows, is that the effort of pursuing them with true Socratic determination is rewarded only by painstaking discovery of one's own puzzlement at how to answer them, and the suspicion that it may not be possible to answer them at all – at least, not in the quite general and decontextualised form in which they were originally raised.

Worse still, if 'What is writing?' is not immediately dismissed either as a trivial question or as an unanswerable one, it begins to sound like a question which, taken seriously,

[1] Thomas Astle, *The Origin and Progress of Writing*, London, 1784, p.1.

requires a formidably long and complex answer. It may seem, for example, to call for an account of the world's many and diverse writing systems. It may equally seem to call for a discussion of literacy; and the psychology of literacy is a topic which might fill several volumes, to say nothing of the sociology of literacy.[2] Do we need to go into all this before we can begin to tackle the problem of the origin of writing? We might hope not. Nevertheless, it remains true that unless a reasonably clear answer can be given to the question 'What is writing?' there is simply no basis on which to propose any solution to the problem of its origin.

The difficulty standing in the way of giving that 'satisfactory account' which Thomas Astle wanted is also in part due to conflation with accounts of related but different matters. How, when, what and where human beings first wrote are ultimately questions for the archaeologist and the philologist. They are questions which may never be answered with absolute certainty, and this book does not claim to be able to provide any new facts which add to the corpus of those already known. But the origin of writing is a different question, and it does not fall either to the archaeologist or to the philologist to answer it. As with many other problems concerning origins, the experts on ancient civilisations have not been backward in providing theories. But before evidence from history can be brought to bear on the question, there has to be some assurance that it actually is evidence. If the archaeologist and the philologist are to distinguish between what is relevant and what is not, a critical examination is required of the question being asked and the way it should be posed. Neglect of this preliminary critical examination is what has been mainly responsible for the widespread acceptance of historical 'answers' which are not answers at all.

[2] See, for example, H.J. Graff, *Literacy in History*, Chicago, 1976; J. Goody (ed.) *Literacy in Traditional Societies*, Cambridge, 1968; E.A. Havelock, *Origins of Western Literacy*, Toronto, 1976, and *The Literate Revolution in Ancient Greece and its Cultural Consequences*, Princeton, 1982.

One reason, indeed, why the origin of writing is such an absorbing question is that the way it has usually been treated illustrates most aptly a conceptual mistake virtually endemic in the Western intellectual tradition. Our carefully cultivated European awareness of languages as unique chronological continuities, each carrying and embodying its own cultural inheritance, has fostered from Graeco-Roman antiquity onward a recurrent tendency to suppose that basic questions concerning language can be given merely historical answers. When history fails to provide the answers, as is inevitably the case, the blame is doubly laid at history's door. In other words, the responsibility for coming up with an answer is handed over to those whose job it is to unearth fresh evidence about the past. The question of the origin of writing provides a classic example of this process. The result is total inability to see that the question is as much a question about our own understanding of language in the present as about the practices of our cultural ancestors in the remote past.

*

The author is indebted to many people other than those mentioned in the main body of the book for suggesting ideas which have found their way – often in a less-than-recognisable form – into the making of his argument. He is especially grateful to Anthony Bladon, Peter Crook, Peter Hacker, Rita Harris, Tony Holiday, Dovid Katz, Nigel Love, John Marshall, Peter Mayer, Peter Mühlhäusler, Malcolm Parkes, Donald Richards and Erica Schumacher. They are not to be blamed for the use he has made of their suggestions.

R.H.

Acknowledgments

The author and publisher wish to thank the following for supplying and giving permission to reproduce illustrations:

Ashmolean Museum, Oxford, pp. 4, 18, 33
Bodleian Library, Oxford, pp. 128, 153
British Library, London, pp. 21, 22, 23
British Museum, pp. 77, 79
Egyptian National Museum, Cairo, pp. 68, 69
Institut Royal des Sciences Naturelles de Belgique, Brussels, p. 136
Lawrence Hill & Co, Connecticut, p. 134
Lowe and Howard-Spink, p. 149
Musée du Louvre, Paris, p. 70
Oxford University Phonetics Laboratory, p. 94
Phaidon Picture Archive, p. 54
US Library of Congress, Washington DC, p. 14

Chapter One

From Folklore to Technology

Once upon a most early time was a Neolithic man. He was not a Jute or an Angle, or even a Dravidian, which he might well have been, Best Beloved, but never mind why. He was a Primitive, and he lived cavily in a Cave, and he wore very few clothes, and he couldn't read and he couldn't write and he didn't want to, and except when he was hungry he was quite happy.

Thus begins the well-known account of the origin of writing which became familiar to generations of English-speaking children and their parents through the ritual reading of Kipling's *Just So Stories*.[1] In 'How the first letter was written' we are told about the fishing expedition when young Taffimai first hit upon the idea of sending a message to her mother by means of scratching a drawing upon a piece of birch bark. The objective was to explain that her father Tegumai had broken the spear he was using to catch carp in the river, and needed a new one. But the drawing was misinterpreted by Taffimai's mother, who thought it meant that her husband had been attacked by a band of hostile warriors and needed the tribe's help. The ensuing confusion was great. When it was all over, however, the chief of the tribe congratulated little Taffimai on her efforts at birch-bark communication with these memorable words: 'It *is* a great invention, and some day men will call it writing.'

With the diachronic wisdom typical of the best of Kipling's characters, the chief of Taffimai's tribe added for good measure the prophecy that:

[1] First edition, London, 1902.

a time will come, O Babe of Tegumai, when we shall make letters – all twenty-six of 'em, – and when we shall be able to read as well as to write, and then we shall always say exactly what we mean without any mistakes.[2]

What the wise chief could not then have foreseen was that the invention of the alphabet was only a week away, as we learn in the next story ('How the alphabet was made'[3]). Here Taffimai designs the letter A by choosing the picture of a carp with its mouth wide open to represent what her father looks like when uttering the sound 'ah'. The letter O is chosen as the egg-or-stone shape to match the shape of her father's mouth when he says 'oh'. The letter S represents a snake, and stands for the hissing sound the snake makes. Altogether, it takes Taffimai and Tegumai just two days to complete an inventory of sound-symbols adequate to spell any word in their language.

Unlike his children's stories about how the camel got its hump and the elephant its trunk, Kipling's aetiological account in this instance embodies certain ingredients of a conventional wisdom upon the subject which had long been accepted in the Western intellectual tradition. Among these one may note: (i) the assumption that speech existed before writing, (ii) the assumption that written messages were originally communicational substitutes for spoken messages, (iii) the assumption that writing began as an attempt at pictorial representation, (iv) the assumption that the alphabet is based on quite a different principle from that of 'picture writing', (v) the assumption that alphabetic symbols are attempts to indicate sounds, and (vi) the assumption that the adoption of the alphabetic principle marks an improvement over 'picture writing'. These assumptions can all be traced back to Classical antiquity, and they proved to be assumptions which were to provide the entire conceptual framework for inquiry into the

[2] *Just So Stories*, London, repr. 1984, p. 129.
[3] ibid. pp.133-49.

origin of writing for the next two thousand years and more. Where the Classical account differs historically from Kipling's is that it points back not to Neolithic tribes but only as far as the Egypt of the pharaohs.

It was the founder of the 26th dynasty, Psamtik or Psammetichos who, if we are to believe Herodotus (2.2), must take the credit for showing the first signs of scientific curiosity about the linguistic prehistory of mankind. He gave instructions that two newborn babies were to be isolated and brought up without hearing anyone speak in their presence during their infancy.[4] His purpose was to discover what first words they would utter if not influenced by the instruction and example of their parents or others. This, he supposed, might produce evidence relevant to determining which was the oldest language in the world. Apocryphal or not, the tale has a symbolic ring to it which ensured its preservation for posterity. Similar experiments were subsequently attributed to Frederick II of Germany, James IV of Scotland and the Moghul emperor Akbar Khan. The symbolic attraction of the story lies in the attempt to probe in the present a mystery forever hidden in the mists of time: the origin of speech.

No parallel story has come down to us from antiquity about attempts to discover the origin of writing. The lacuna is of some significance. The obvious explanation would be that in antiquity the question of the origin of writing was not regarded as equally mysterious; and in support of this there is no lack of evidence. Pharaoh Psammetichos may well have been perplexed by the seemingly arbitrary correlation of spoken sounds with meanings; but he could hardly have wondered why the Egyptian hieroglyphs included characters

---

[4] This was achieved by entrusting them to the care of a shepherd, who brought them up in a remote hut. Thus psycholinguistics got off to a bad start by attempting what psychologists of the twentieth century call a 'deprivation experiment'. A nastier version, also mentioned by Herodotus, was that the pharaoh had their foster mothers' tongues cut out.

Hieroglyphic writing. Stela of Iuny, Chief King's Scribe, and of his wife, Renut. XIXth Dynasty, *c.* 1250 B.C. Ashmolean Museum, Oxford.

recognisable as the shape of an owl, or a snake, or a leg. Here there was no call for experimental investigation. The explanation must surely be that writing originated as drawing. This, at least, was the explanation already taken for granted by Greek and Roman writers. As Diodorus Siculus (3.4) puts it in the first century B.C., the Egyptian hieroglyphic signs 'take the shape of animals of every kind and of the members of the human body, and of implements ... For their writing does not express the intended concept by means of syllables joined one to another but by means of the significance of the objects which have been copied ... '[5] In similar vein, Tacitus tells us (*Annals* 11. 14.) that the Egyptians were the first people to devise a way of representing mental concepts by animal drawings.

Given these pictorial beginnings, all that remained to explain was whether the alphabet was an independent and unconnected invention, or whether it was simply a later development or corruption of picture writing. In any case, the Egyptians gave themselves credit for the alphabet as well (although, as Tacitus tells us, there were rival claimants, in particular the Phoenicians). But no one challenged the historical priority of the hieroglyphs or their manifestly pictorial character.

How little the opinion of scholars had changed by the time we reach the eighteenth century may be gauged from Joseph Priestley's *Lectures on the Theory of Language and Universal Grammar.*[6] According to Priestley, 'both natural probability and history show that *picture-writing*, with the contraction of it into *Hieroglyphics*'[7] preceded alphabetic writing. As to the origin of picture-writing and its subsequent evolution, nothing could be plainer in Priestley's estimation.

To express a tree, or animal, they who first used this method would probably begin in the most simple manner, by drawing an actual sketch or outline of the tree or animal, and proceed in like manner to depict all other visible objects ... By degrees they would learn to contract these pictures, and only to draw so

[5] Tr.C.H. Oldfather, Loeb Classical Library, London, 1935.
[6] Warrington, 1762.
[7] ibid., p.32.

much of their first outline as was sufficient to distinguish one expression from another. Thus *two swords*, and then *two cross-strokes* would serve to express a *battle*: which was at first represented by the figures of men in a fighting posture; and to denote impossibility, a plain horizontal line might suffice for the water, and two upright strokes for feet, & c.[8]

Evidently it no more occurred to Priestley than it occurred to Diodorus Siculus that there was anything wanting in this kind of explanation.

Thus the first and most enduring obscurity about the origin of writing is engendered, paradoxically, by its not being treated at first as problematic at all (unlike the question of the origin of speech). Not until comparatively recent times do we find an allegorisation of the problem which matches in imaginative impact the story of Pharaoh Psammetichos' experiment. The *locus classicus* is early twentieth-century, and bound up with the popular recognition of modern civilisation's psychological debt to its primitive forebears. It was bound to feature (where else?) in that archetypally Darwinian myth of the human condition which is the story of Tarzan of the Apes.

Tarzan was at first puzzled, as readers of Edgar Rice Burroughs will recall, by the rows of little 'bugs' which crawled across the pages of the illustrated book discovered in the late Lord Greystoke's log cabin. But not for long. With his true English aristocrat's keen intelligence unblunted by a public school education, Tarzan eventually worked out for himself what the little bugs must be. He not only discovered what various individual bugs meant, but taught himself to draw them as well. Having mastered the bugs, he held – although little realising it at the time – the key to unlock the storehouse of all human knowledge. Thus Tarzan tackling single-handed the great mystery of writing presents, as his creator takes care to tell us, in case we had missed it,

[8] ibid., pp.32-4.

an allegorical figure of the primordial groping through the black night of ignorance towards the light of learning.[9]

It takes a linguistic theorist to misread the allegory and dismiss it as reflecting the way literate societies naively assign priority to the written word, treating the spoken word as its derivative.[10] We may well agree that Tarzan's was a remarkable feat 'beside which the decipherment of Egyptian, Old Persian, Sumerian, Hieroglyphic Hittite and Linear B must be considered child's play';[11] but that is not quite the point. The book Tarzan discovers is not just any old book; it is a primer containing the alphabet.

The symbolism of that discovery as pointing the way to the 'light of learning' is profound. For just as the book from which Tarzan learns is not any old book, so too the alphabet is not any old writing system. The alphabet, for Western civilisation, is the writing system *par excellence*. It represents writing brought to its highest pitch of perfection, towards which less 'advanced' systems were in turn clumsily groping. Noteworthy too is the detail that Tarzan first encounters the alphabet in its most sophisticated manifestation. For not only is the alphabet in his primer both means and end, a writing system used in the service of its own propagation, but it is presented to this youthful inquirer in its most technically advanced guise; that is to say, in its printed form. The mechanical regularity of print confers upon each alphabetic symbol an independence and a constant visual identity which no earlier form of writing quite achieves. Print, in Marshall McLuhan's phrase, is the supreme 'ditto device'.[12] It eliminates the personal expressiveness of handwriting in favour of automatic uniformity. Thus in Tarzan's first confrontation with the mystery of writing there

---

[9] Edgar Rice Burroughs, *Tarzan of the Apes*, New York, 1912; repr. 1984, p.48.

[10] F.W. Householder, *Linguistic Speculations*, Cambridge, 1971, Ch.13.

[11] ibid., p.247.

[12] *The Medium is the Massage*, New York, 1967, p.50.

is a dual contrast: it opposes not only the preliterate to the literate, but the pre-mechanical to the civilisation of the machine. The printed book symbolises simultaneously the power of the techniques which literacy makes available, and the resultant realisation of the full potential of writing as an instrument of communication.

The significance of the fact that in teaching himself to read Tarzan simply bypasses speech (for he has no idea of how English is pronounced) is not a symbolic assertion of the unimportance of the spoken word. What it means is that, as befits a representative of the primordial, Tarzan brings initially to the task of mastering the alphabet a more primitive concept of writing then the alphabetic concept. This, combined with the fact that Tarzan has no teacher to guide his efforts at self-instruction, turns the allegory of decipherment into a parable about the origin of writing itself. To begin, as Tarzan's book does, with

A is for Archer

is to begin at the end; or, at least, the end of the beginning. For like Tarzan, the originators of writing did not fully grasp, doubtless, what it was they had taught themselves to do.

Perhaps, then, it should not come as too much of a surprise to us to discover that we do not seem to understand it either. But our surprise is the arrogant surprise of modernity; and we pay for the arrogance by our failure to be shocked by the word-order of a cultural formula like 'A is for Archer'. Should it not go 'Archer is for A'? That at least would fit in better with the so-called 'acrophonic' process by which, according to most authorities, the alphabet itself evolved from a pre-alphabetic phase of human writing. We all have our own personal versions of Tarzan's primer. (A is not for Archer according to some, but for Apple.) Just how many such alphabetic labyrinths there are for destiny and nursery school to force the human child through towards literacy probably no one knows. That, however, is idle curiosity. Less idle is the curiosity which might prompt us to try to recall what, as children, we first made of these formulae. For it seems that to stand a chance of understanding them, we must already be familiar with the information they summarise. Otherwise, to be taught the formulae is simply to be taught a jingle: and that is doubtless how it is, or was, for many a child. Right at the alphabetic beginning we are plunged into ritual.

Formulae of this kind have a special communicational status. They fall into the class which Wittgenstein in the *Tractatus* calls *Erläuterungen* ('elucidations'). They are not statements or elucidations in any ordinary sense, because they are 'propositions that contain the primitive signs. So they can only be understood if the meanings of those signs are already known'.[13] Thus we ought to be able to make as much or as little sense of it if the formula were not 'A is for Archer' but, let us suppose, 'C is for Archer'. After all, there is only one *c* in *archer*, just as there is only one *a*; and visually it would probably be no less convincing in the child's imagination. It does not take much artistic flair to design a primer which shows us the *c* as an archer's bow at full stretch. But a fairly safe bet on cultural universals would be to wager that no society familiar with writing constructs alphabetic mnemonics on any other than the 'A is for Archer' model. 'Archer is for A', 'C is for Archer', 'A is for 'Orses' and other imaginable perversions are just that: perversions. To grasp that fact is to take at least a first step toward articulating the developmental psychology of *homo alphabeticus*. 'A is for Archer' it has to be, because in the beginning was not the Word, according to the Bible of Alphabetic Man. In the beginning was the Letter.

With historical hindsight, we can see that Tarzan takes up the problem of writing at just the point where Diodorus

---

[13] L. Wittgenstein, *Tractatus Logico-Philosophicus*, tr.ed. D.F. Pears and B.F. McGuinness, London, 2nd ed., 1971, § 3.263.

Siculus, Tacitus and the world of antiquity left it. It is the problem of bridging the gap between pictorial and non-pictorial modes of visual expression. Tarzan never for a moment entertains the possibility that bugs and pictures might be totally unrelated. Furthermore, he treats the pictures in his primer as entirely unproblematic, except insofar as they represent things he has never himself seen the like of. Similarly, modern scholarship has taken for granted that somehow the emergence of non-pictorial scripts must be explicable by reference to the prior existence of pictorial forms of communication, themselves treated as unproblematic in principle. It is that primary conception – or misconception – of what needs explaining which the Tarzan story captures.

*

Accounts of the origin of writing fall into two categories: the magical and the rational. In both Kipling and Burroughs, for all the picturesque elements of fantasy, we find an account which is basically of the rational type. For ultimately the explanation offered is an explanation in terms of human ingenuity. But magical versions are often no less interesting. Their appeal to the supernatural may capture attitudes towards writing which do not easily lend themselves to rationalisation.

Typical is a Blackfoot Indian legend about how the secret of writing was first revealed to the Blackfoot people. The revelation, as Chief Buffalo Child Long Lance tells it in his autobiography,[14] was brought by the spirit Boy Thunder to one chosen member of the tribe. His name was Mokuyi-Kinasi (Wolf Head). As a youth, he was struck by lightning during a thunder storm, and thereafter became one of the most powerful medicine men in the Blackfoot nation. One day a missionary came to tell the Blackfoot about the white man's Great Spirit, and to learn the Blackfoot language so that he

[14] *Long Lance*, Alberta, 1928.

could devise a writing system for it. It was then that Boy
Thunder appeared to Wolf Head in a dream and hung a large
buffalo hide on the wall of his tepee. The hide was covered
with strange markings and Boy Thunder asked Wolf Head if
he knew what they were. When Wolf Head said he did not,
Boy Thunder told him that each line of marks was a different
language in writing. Then Wolf Head was asked if he could
understand any of the marks, but he could not. Boy Thunder
told him to keep on looking hard at the hide, and eventually
Wolf Head discovered a line of marks down one of the legs of
the buffalo skin which he was able to understand, and
recognised it as the Blackfoot language put into writing. Boy
Thunder told him that from then on he would be able to
understand Blackfoot writing. The next morning, Wolf Head
went to the missionary and amazed all by writing in the
Blackfoot syllabary which the missionary had devised but had
not yet taught to anyone. The missionary in question was
Archdeacon Tims, and when Long Lance was writing in 1928
Wolf Head was still living on the Blackfoot Reservation at
Gleichen, Alberta. He had reached the venerable age of 83,
but had lost all his former powers as a medicine man on
becoming converted to Christianity.

It does not take a great deal of pondering upon this tale to
see that its folklore purpose is, as it were, to snatch a mythical
last-minute victory over the white man and give the Blackfoot
credit for the introduction of Blackfoot writing. It achieves an
honourable compromise between national pride and history.
Since there is no plausible historical reason to explain the
sudden and independent invention of writing by a hitherto
illiterate people, the supernatural intervention of a Blackfoot
spirit is invoked to account for it. Crucial to the story is the
feature that Mokuyi-Kinasi has no need to learn anything
from the missionary: he is simply able to 'recognise' Blackfoot
writing when he looks at it carefully, and understand it
without explanation. This mystical 'recognition', and not the
labours of Archdeacon Tims, is what authenticates the writing

as genuine Blackfoot writing.

There is a great deal which might be said, in the context of this Blackfoot legend, concerning the psychology of an appeal to the 'recognition' of writing. On one level, the recognition demanded is recognition of the independence and autonomy of Blackfoot writing, which links up in obvious ways with the sense in which one 'recognises' claims to human rights and cultural self-determination. On another level, recognition is a metaphor drawn from the reading process itself, which requires a certain visual pattern to be seen as the instantiation of units in a given script. On a third level, what is significant is that although recognition normally presupposes prior identification of and acquaintance with the thing recognised, no institution of a whole convention of recognition can be explained in this way. This is exactly the case with the origin of any script; or with the origin of writing itself. In these instances, there is a sense in which the experience of recognition is primary, and the identification of what exactly it is that has been recognised is secondary and subsequent. This psychological aspect of the genesis of a whole new social institution is the aspect brilliantly captured in the story of Wolf Head. Since modern social psychology has no 'rational' explanation for phenomena of this order either, it is inevitable that they should be comprehended, if comprehended at all, under the guise of magic and the supernatural.

All this, however, stands in the sharpest contrast with the well-attested invention in the early nineteenth century of the Cherokee syllabary by the Indian Sequoyah – otherwise known as John Giss, Guest or Guess – the only person in history known to have achieved literacy by inventing a complete writing system single-handed.[15] In one sense Sequoyah out-Tarzaned Tarzan; but in another sense, unlike Tarzan, he merely copied others. Sequoyah made no secret of his ambition to emulate the white man and make available to

[15] Grant Foreman, *Sequoyah*, Oklahoma, 1938.

his own people the magic of the white man's 'talking leaves'. Although he knew no English he did not hesitate to borrow shapes from the English alphabet and assign Cherokee phonetic values to them. Thus, for example, Sequoyah's character M represents the sound 'lu', while S represents the sound 'du'. A score or more of the 85 characters in his syllabary are recognisable English letters, incorporated alongside other symbols of his own design.

What is even more interesting is that according to one contemporary witness[16] Sequoyah's interest in the matter was originally sparked by a dispute among his fellow Cherokees as to whether the 'talking leaves' were the invention of the white man or the gift of the Great Spirit. General opinion favoured attribution to the Great Spirit, but Sequoyah championed the less popular view that writing was merely a human invention. His subsequent production of a syllabary for Cherokee may perhaps be seen as a determined attempt to vindicate the thesis that the magic of the talking leaves was not magic but just ingenuity.

Sequoyah, however, was clearly a quite exceptional figure in the history of the subject. The theory he rejected, which attributes the invention of the art of writing to non-human or superhuman agencies of various kinds, is enshrined in mythology the world over. One Chinese legend gives the credit to a sacred turtle. Monkeys, according to the Ekoi of Nigeria, taught their ancestors the original symbols of the Nsibidi script. (It may be no coincidence that the patron deity of scribes in ancient Egypt was represented as a baboon.) In early India, the Middle East and Europe, various divinities (Brahma, Nebo, Thoth, Isis, Hermes) were said to have invented writing. In more recent times, the Vai syllabary of Liberia and the Bamoun script of the Cameroons were both claimed to have been revealed to their inventors in dreams or visions.

[16] ibid., p.20.

Contemporary portrait by Charles Bird King of Sequoyah explaining characters in his Cherokee syllabary. U.S. Library of Congress.

Such accounts thrive no doubt upon the naive awe of illiterate populations for the enigmatic and occult aspects of writing (fostered in all probability by the privileged few who held the key to writing in their own hands); but they may also reflect a more deep-seated psychological acknowledgment that writing is one of those arts which goes beyond the naturally endowed capacities of the human being. If speech itself already distinguishes human beings from all other living creatures, writing goes one stage further. For whereas every child who is not in some way handicapped will normally learn to speak, there have been whole communities, whole cultures which did not know – and could scarcely have imagined – what it is to be able to write.

Of the thousands of languages spoken at different periods in different parts of the globe, fewer than one in ten have ever developed an indigenous written form. Of these, the number to have produced a significant body of literature barely exceeds one hundred. But it is not only its comparative rarity as a cultural achievement which makes of writing something impressive and awe-inspiring. The Cherokee phrase 'talking leaves' expresses more brilliantly than many scholarly monographs the seemingly miraculous element in writing. Leaves of paper have no voice; and yet they can be made to speak. But the miracle by which this is accomplished is conceptually difficult to grasp in all its complexity and, paradoxically, all the more so for people who take reading and writing for granted as part of the normal course of education. Literacy scorns the 'base degrees by which it did ascend'; it leaves little room for the mystery of writing, which finds its apt expression in the name early given to the symbols of the old Teutonic alphabet. They are called *runes*: and etymologically the term means 'secret'.

What is commonly held to be the only reference to writing in Homer is significant too. It occurs in the story of Bellerophon and King Proitos,[17] which turns up later in European literature as Claudius' attempt to get rid of Hamlet in Shakespeare's play. The mechanism of the story is simple. An unwanted person is sent on a journey to deliver a message. The message, of which the bearer is ignorant, instructs the recipient to kill the messenger. Here we see, it has been suggested, both the awe of the pre-literate mind for literacy, and the primitive superstition which treats writing as a magic

[17] *Iliad* 6. 160ff.

art.[18] Certainly, it is a story which requires the technology of writing, or something equivalent. For merely to instruct a messenger *viva voce* to tell another person to kill him would defeat its own object. One is reminded here of the ancient and no less superstitious practice of killing the slave who brought bad tidings. Writing is the mysterious technology by which any message may be concealed from its illiterate bearer.

It would take a dull mind to count it a mere accident that the three most common representations of Bellerophon in the art of antiquity are Bellerophon slaying the Chimaera, Bellerophon with his famous horse Pegasus, and Bellerophon leaving Argos with the letter. For the first two are subjects of intrinsic visual interest; whereas leaving with a letter is, to say the least, visually unexciting. Why then is it an episode so worthy of artistic perpetuation?

The allegory of Bellerophon's letter is no less profound than that of Tarzan's bugs. The two are complementary. In both, writing appears as a mystery which stands between the individual and an understanding of his own fate. (For which, read: a mystery which separates pre-literate mankind from true knowledge. Without that exteriorisation and objectivity which writing captures, knowledge – even self-knowledge – might be a transient illusion.)

Part of the mystery is this. Although writing intrinsically requires visual interpretation, script does not reveal its secrets to mere inspection. Not only is an unfamiliar script meaningless to the beholder, but it is not even obvious to the naked – or innocent – eye (the two are often assumed to be the same) what constitutes writing and what does not. Writing, perplexing as it may seem, has no distinctively visual characteristics by which it may be identified. A Western tourist on a first visit to the Taj Mahal may well fail to recognise that the bands of inlaid stone across the facade fall into two distinct categories. Some of these bands are

---

[18] W. Leaf, *The Iliad*, 2nd ed., London, 1900, Vol.1, p.270.

Koranic text on the Taj Mahal, India.

intricately stylised floral motifs. Others are texts from the
Koran. A visitor who knows nothing at all about Arabic may
not be able to tell one from the other. The same holds if we
substitute for the Taj Mahal a Mayan stela of the ninth
century A.D. When we first encounter an unknown script,
there may be nothing to tell us that it is a script at all. For its
most conspicuous visual features will be shared by patterns
which are not – or may not be – scripts. These other patterns
may be man-made, or they may be the result of natural
processes. Before the decipherment of Persian cuneiform,
sceptics held that there was no such script, on the ground that
the marks which excited the attention and ingenuity of
philologists could have been made by birds walking at random
across newly soft clay. The implausibility of this theory does
not rob the story of its point. Although he did not think birds
were likely to have produced these patterns, even the Oxford
professor who coined the term *cuneiform* thought they were

Neo-Sumerian cuneiform. Baked clay prism with dynastic table of the kings of Sumer and Akkad, *c.* 1817 B.C. Ashmolean Museum, Oxford.

decorative fantasies devised by Persian architects.[19]

Granted the superficially mysterious nature of script, it may be taken as a landmark of intellectual maturity in civilised attitudes towards writing to discover the first signs of scepticism concerning literacy. They are to be found surprisingly early in the Western tradition.

Socrates, in Plato's dialogue *Phaedrus*, tells the story of the ancient Egyptian god Thoth who invented various arts, including writing, and sought approval of his inventions from the king of Egypt. The king thought some of Thoth's inventions were good and others bad. When it came to writing, Thoth said: 'This invention, O king, will make the Egyptians wiser and will improve their memories; for it is an elixir of memory and wisdom that I have discovered.' But the king was not impressed, and replied: 'You, who are the father of letters, have been led by your affection to ascribe to them a power the opposite of that which they really possess. For this invention will produce forgetfulness in the minds of those who learn to use it, because they will not practise their memory. Their trust in writing, produced by external characters which are no part of themselves, will discourage the use of their own memory within them. You have invented an elixir not of memory, but of reminding; and you offer your pupils the appearance of wisdom, not true wisdom, for they will read many things without instruction and will therefore seem to know many things, when they are for the most part ignorant ... '[20] Socrates is later accused of making this account up; but who made it up makes little difference for our present purposes. Clearly Sequoyah, if he had ever heard the story, did not feel that these objections detracted from the desirability of making the practical advantages of the 'talking

---

[19] The professor was Thomas Hyde, who published his *Historia religionis veterum Persarum* in 1700. On Hyde's 'proof' that the inscriptions could not be writing, see M. Pope, *The Story of Decipherment*, London, 1975, p.88.

[20] *Phaedrus* 274-5, tr. H.N. Fowler, Loeb Classical Library, London, 1914.

leaves' available to the Cherokee nation.

Nor were the king of Egypt's misgivings about writing shared by those who subsequently shaped the patterns of European education. For once the Greeks had perfected the alphabet in basically the form we know today, and the Romans had adapted it to Latin, writing rapidly became the basis of both elementary and advanced learning throughout Europe. It has remained so down to the present century. More generally, the invention of which Thoth was so proud – whether or not the credit is rightly his – has come to be acclaimed as one of the greatest technological advances ever made in human history.

'More profound in its own way than the discovery of fire or the wheel' is how one authority describes the impact of writing on the course of human history.[21] 'More important than all the battles ever fought', says another.[22] H.G. Wells in his *Short History of the World* summed up the significance of writing for mankind as follows:

> It put agreements, laws, commandments on record. It made the growth of states larger than the old city states possible. It made a continuous historical consciousness possible. The command of the priest or king and his seal could go far beyond his sight and voice and could survive his death.[23]

These are typical twentieth-century acknowledgments of the technological importance of writing.

The claims Wells makes are substantial. But they could be amply illustrated from English history alone. Perhaps the best known examples of the administrative and political poten-tialities of writing, for Englishmen, are the Domesday Book of 1086 and Magna Carta of 1215 respectively. In both cases the

---

[21] D. Diringer, *Writing*, London, 1961, p.19.
[22] J.H. Breasted, *The Conquest of Civilisation*, New York, 1926, p.54.
[23] H.G. Wells, *A Short History of the World*, rev.ed. 1946, Harmondsworth, p.49.

Magna Carta, 1215. British Library.

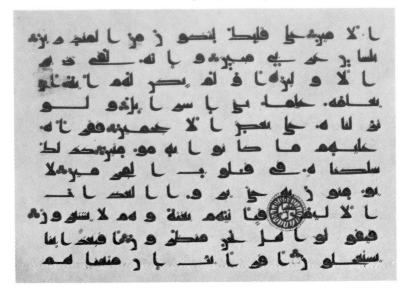

The Koran, surah xxvi, verses 193-204. Tenth-century manuscript in Kufic script. British Library Or. MS 1397, f.15b.

written record secured an institutional authority which would have been impossible without writing. A more dramatic attestation, however, comes from the Arabic tradition. When in 633 A.D. many of the Ḥuffāẓ (those who had memorised the Prophet's revelations and could recite them from memory) were killed in the battles that followed the death of the prophet Muhammed, 'Umar ibn al-Khaṭṭāb urged the first Caliph, Abū Bakr, to commit the text of the Koran to writing.[24] This excellent piece of advice was followed, and as a result the Koran passed into history as one of the great sacred books of the world.

Wells might have added that even as late as the twentieth century the political and economic structure of the modern world, with its strikingly uneven distribution of wealth, facilities and resources, both as between individuals and as between states, can still be seen as a reflection of the length of

[24] Y.H. Safadi, *Islamic Calligraphy*, London, 1978, p.9.

Printing: the second revolution in communication. The 42-line Bible, Mainz, *c.* 1453-5. British Library.

time it took different social groups to realise and exploit fully the advantages of writing as a system of communication. It is not by chance that today the global maps of illiteracy and poverty so nearly coincide.

The 'writing revolution' was the first of the great communication revolutions in the history of mankind. The next came several thousand years later, with the advent of printing, followed after a much shorter interval by the development of telegraphy and telephony. But writing had been the world's most advanced communications technology from the fourth millennium B.C. down to the fifteenth century A.D. Wells puts his finger on the reasons why. Writing set human communication free from the limitations imposed by the impermanence of speech, and dispensed with the live presence of a speaker. It made verbal communication independent of the individual communicator, by providing an autonomous text which could survive transmission over time and distance. What is interesting is that these are precisely the reasons why the king of Egypt – at least, according to Socrates – condemned the invention of writing. It divorced verbal communication from the original efforts and intentions implicit in face-to-face speech.

The writing revolution was not merely of political and economic significance. The autonomous text was naturally suited to become the basis not only of law but of education and literature. Anthropologists and sociologists nowadays recognise no more fundamental distinction that that which separates literate from preliterate cultures, and the differences are manifest in countless details of social organisation and institutions. More speculatively, it has been claimed that writing profoundly affected the way people came to think and to argue: that it brought in its wake a restructuring of human mental processes.[25] Even Plato with his professed scepticism

---

[25] W.J. Ong, *Orality and Literacy*, London, 1982; esp. Ch.4, 'Writing restructures consciousness'.

about the value of writing and his emphasis on *viva voce* exchange relied heavily, it has been claimed, on modes of discourse and presentation which would have been out of the question without the underlying support of the written word. The careful organisation of a Socratic dialogue, let alone the organisation of connexions between one dialogue and another, is the kind of organisation which not even a Plato can undertake without at least jotting down a few notes. The complexity of a long, articulated chain of rational argument cannot simply be 'carried in the head'. The mind's eye needs to be able to scan discussion before it can plan discussion on that kind of scale, just as an architect needs drawings as soon as his projected buildings go beyond a certain level of simplicity, or a composer needs musical notation. As I.D. Bent points out, it is extremely doubtful whether the operas of Wagner could have been composed, let alone performed, without the resources of notation. 'It enables the composer to shape his work to a level of sophistication that is impossible in a purely oral tradition.'[26]

Since the importance of writing is now so widely recognised in these various respects, it is ironic that the origin of writing remains obscure. The obscurity is only partly – and least importantly – due to lack of historical evidence. A more crucial matter is the way the problem itself has been conceived or misconceived by modern scholarship.

There are a number of reasons for this, among which five stand out. One is the fact that the recognition of the importance of writing has focused upon the *consequences* which the use of writing subsequently brought about in the development of civilisation. This attention to the consequences has meant that writing is contrasted with and seen as an extension of the earlier mode of communication which it partially replaced; namely, speech. Functionally, it is true that

---

[26] *The New Grove Dictionary of Music and Musicians*, London, 1980, vol.13, 'Notation', p.334.

writing may become an extension of speech; but technically it is not. From a technical point of view, writing is an extension of drawing, or more generally of graphic art, if we subsume under that term the whole gamut of forms of colouring, carving, incision and impression of surfaces which writing employs. For many scholars, this technical legacy of graphic art is seen as being of importance only for its consequences: in other words because it opened up the possibility of making permanent verbal records for human use. But the connexion of writing with graphic art is of more fundamental significance than this, as the following chapters will try to show.

A second reason is that a long line of influential thinkers, from Plato and Aristotle onwards, have treated writing simply as a representation of speech. Aristotle in *De Interpretatione* (1.4-6) says: 'Words spoken are symbols or signs of affections or impressions of the soul; written words are the signs of words spoken.'[27] The Aristotelian view is echoed in the eighteenth century by Rousseau, and by the twentieth has become no longer one possible view but an 'accepted fact'. Thus we find the eleventh edition of *Encyclopaedia Britannica* giving a definition of writing as 'the use of letters, symbols or other conventional characters, for the recording by visible means of significant sounds.'[28] The position is one endorsed by a number of major theorists of modern linguistics from Saussure down to the present day. Saussure says: 'A language and its written form constitute two separate systems of signs. The sole reason for the existence of the latter is to represent the former.'[29] For Bloomfield writing is 'merely a way of recording language.'[30] Both Saussure and Bloomfield equate languages with spoken languages and produce these observations about the relationship between spoken and

[27] Tr. H.P. Cook, Loeb Classical Library, London, 1938, p.115.
[28] Vol. 28, p.852 (1911).
[29] F. de Saussure, *Course in General Linguistics*, tr. R. Harris, London, 1983, p.24.
[30] L. Bloomfield, *Language*, London, 1935, p.21.

written forms as factual statements rather than as theses which need to be argued for. It would be more appropriate, however, to place them among the postulates of linguistic theory: for one can see, as Derrida puts it,

> in the very movement by which linguistics is instituted as a science, a metaphysical presupposition about the relationship between speech and writing.[31]

This view of writing as 'a symbol of a symbol, or symbolism twice removed'[32] may perhaps seem plausible if one tacitly equates writing with the actual or potential use of the alphabet, as Aristotle probably did (Greek civilisation having given the world the alphabet in its first complete form). However, one thing that the historical record makes abundantly clear, and which may not have been clear to Aristotle, is that the development of the alphabet is a comparatively late event in the evolution of writing. Various civilisations with a long history of writing never developed systems comparable to the alphabet. So alphabetic representation of articulated sounds is actually an irrelevance as far as the origin of writing is concerned. There is no evidence that anywhere in the world writing began with the alphabet, and plenty of evidence that it did not. Once one sees the fallacy of equating writing with alphabetic writing, the whole question of the extent to which and the sense in which writing is a representation of speech at all becomes more debatable than Aristotle, or modern Aristotelians, would acknowledge.

A third – and perhaps the most important – reason why the problem of the origin of writing may be misconstrued is that it is posed, inevitably, from the point of view of a civilisation which has already assimilated writing and its consequences. It takes a considerable effort of imagination to attempt to set aside retrospectively the assumptions of a literate society and

---

[31] J. Derrida, *Of Grammatology*, tr. G.C. Spivak, Baltimore, 1976, p.28.
[32] J. Whatmough, *Language*, New York, 1956, p.112.

see the question of the origin of writing as it would have appeared to its pre-literate originators. Whoever they were, writing could not have been from the very beginning for them what writing has subsequently come to be for us. Consequently it is a mistake to situate the problem in the context of the earliest surviving forms of what we would nowadays recognise as scripts, whether alphabetic or non-alphabetic. Both logically and psychologically the origin of writing poses a different question. It has to do with the communicational universe of pre-literate humanity. Here the story of Tarzan has everything to teach us, and the story of Bellerophon nothing. Tarzan is an explorer: Bellerophon a victim.

A fourth reason is that some theorists in effect beg the question of the origin of writing by adopting an unduly narrow or arbitrary interpretation of what counts as writing. In particular, exaggerated attention is paid to the role of phonetic notation. This is, again, because what is being sought retrospectively in the long history of human symbol-making are the immediate antecedents of the most prestigious modern forms of script, which are alphabetic. This is a failing particularly evident in evolutionary accounts of the origin of writing.

Finally, part of the obscurity which surrounds the origin of writing may be attributed to the highly unsatisfactory terminology in which discussions of the problem are often conducted. Since the issues involved cannot be articulated at all without using a metalanguage of some kind, it is with terminological questions that any fresh attempt to elucidate the origin of writing may most usefully begin.

Chapter Two

The Tyranny of the Alphabet

We say 'As easy as A.B.C.' No one ever said 'As easy as
Chinese ideograms, or Egyptian hieroglyphics.'

A.C. Moorhouse, 1946.

The problem of the terminology in which to discuss the
question of the origin of writing is in large part a problem
created by the tyranny of the alphabet over our modern ways
of thinking about the relation between the spoken and the
written word.

Although Tarzan mastered the art of writing unaided (and
could even write a letter in impeccable English to his beloved
Jane before being able to speak a word of her native
language)[1] he could hardly have realised (unless the
information was contained in Lord Greystoke's dictionary)
that his own apprenticeship to writing corresponded exactly to
the etymology of the word. For he would not have known that
writing was originally merely a term designating the process of
scoring or outlining a shape on a surface of some kind. (In this
very broad sense, writing ought to include drawing, and even
the art of the silhouette. Nowadays it does not, although that
original use of the verb *write* survives in English as late as the
sixteenth century.) Ancient Egyptian had one word meaning
both 'writing' and 'drawing'. Similarly, the Greek verb γράφειν
('to write') originally meant in Homer 'engrave, scratch,
scrape'. The later restriction of such words to designate
alphabetic writing hardly warrants the narrow perspective

[1] Edgar Rice Burroughs, op.cit., pp. 148-9.

adopted by those historians of the subject who take for granted that graphic signs count as writing only when used for purposes which alphabetic writing was later to fulfil.

The various types of sign used in the writing systems of the world are commonly classified as follows: (i) *alphabetic*, (ii) *syllabic*, (iii) *logographic*, (iv) *pictographic*, and (v) *ideographic*. For people educated in the Western tradition, the most familiar of these is the first.

The form of alphabet most widely used at the present day is the English alphabet, comprising twenty-six letters, each of which has a name and an allotted place in a conventional sequence known as 'alphabetical order'. Each of these twenty-six letters has two forms, one called the 'capital' letter and the other the 'small' letter. Different styles of handwriting and different type faces present both series in somewhat different shapes: but this does not affect the identification of the 'same' set of letters. Alphabetic writing may nowadays for all practical purposes be defined as any system of recording which uses this particular inventory of letters, or some historically related variant of it, of which there are many. The edicts of Ashoka in India and the runic monuments of Scandinavia alike employ alphabetic writing, although presenting little obvious similarity in appearance either to each other or to modern English printed characters.

Historically, the alphabet now used for writing English is derived from the Greek alphabet, the word *alphabet* itself combining the names of the first two letters of the Greek alphabet, *alpha* and *beta*, although the term is of Latin, not Greek, origin. The Greek alphabet in turn is known to have been an adaptation of an earlier Phoenician system of writing. This complicated evolution has now been traced in some detail, thanks to the researches of several generations of scholars.[2] All authorities agree that our ancestors' first attempts at writing were not alphabetic.

[2] Perhaps the best account in English is given by D. Diringer, *The Alphabet*, London, 3rd. ed. 1968.

Historians of writing distinguish a number of theories about the origin of the alphabet. These include the so-called 'Egyptian' theory, which derives the alphabet in one way or another from a simplification of various forms of writing known to have been used in Egypt; the 'Cretan' theory, propounded principally by Sir Arthur Evans, which held the alphabet to have originated in Crete and been taken thence to Palestine, and later borrowed by the Phoenicians; and the 'geometric' theory of Sir Flinders Petrie, which traced back the letters of the alphabet to a set of geometric signs which occur in prehistoric inscriptions throughout the Mediterranean area. The modern consensus view, however, favours the North Semitic alphabet as the earliest known form and dates its appearance to the first half of the second millennium B.C.[3] A more contentious assumption is that the alphabet represents the end-product of a process often called the 'acrophonic principle'. 'According to this principle,' writes Gelb, 'the sign values originated by using the first part of a word expressed in the word sign and by casting off the rest, as if we chose, for example, a picture of a house to stand for *h* because "house" starts with an *h*'.[4]

Alphabetic writing is usually contrasted with an earlier type of writing now generally called *syllabic*. As this term implies, in syllabic writing each sign normally stands for one or more syllables, the inventory of such signs being termed a *syllabary*. Whereas a typical alphabetic system will employ, for instance, three letters to render the English monosyllabic word *sat*, a typical syllabary would have a single sign for that purpose. Syllabaries such as the Japanese, in which each sign has the value of either a single vowel (e.g. *a*) or else a syllable consisting of a combination of consonant followed by a vowel

---

[3] Diringer, op.cit., pp.195-222.
[4] I.J. Gelb, *A Study of Writing*, 2nd. ed., Chicago, 1963, p.143. Gelb himself (p.251.) rejects this explanation and asserts that in his view, with a few sporadic exceptions, 'acrophony as a principle seems to play no part in the history of writing'.

(e.g. *ka, sa, ta, na*) are sometimes called *open syllabaries.* Such syllabaries have no signs for syllables ending in a consonant.

Both alphabetic and syllabic characters are commonly grouped together as *phonograms* (i.e. signs indicating pronunciation). Phonograms are in turn distinguished from three other types of sign: (i) from signs representing a word, but giving no indication of its pronunciation, (ii) from signs which take the form of a simplified picture of the thing they represent, and (iii) from signs representing an idea or a message as a whole, rather than any particular formulation of it. The terms (i) *logogram*, (ii) *pictogram* and (iii) *ideogram* are often used in the senses corresponding respectively to these three distinctions; but not, unfortunately, with ideal consistency. If they were, however, one might give the following illustrative examples: (i) '$' as a *logogram* of the word 'dollar', (ii) a circle with 'rays' radiating from the circumference as a *pictogram* for the sun, and (iii) an arrow mark as an *ideogram* indicating the direction to be followed.[5]

There are two types of sign, both widely employed in writing systems, which do not quite fit into the classification so far described. One of these, which has a foot in both the phonographic and non-phonographic camps, and will be more extensively discussed below, is the *rebus*. The rebus is a transferred pictogram, re-employed as the sign for a word or syllable which by chance happens to be close or identical in pronunciation to the word which originally motivated its pictographic form. Thus, a pictogram originally designating the word *sun*, might subsequently come to be employed as a rebus for the word *son* (assuming, as in these English examples, that the words for 'sun' and 'son' are similarly pronounced in the language in question). The distinctive

---

[5] In China, the traditional classification of written characters recognised no less than six types, including phonograms (*xie sheng*), pictograms (*xiang xing*) and ideograms (*zhi shi*), together with others peculiar to Chinese. (A. Gaur, *A History of Writing*, London, 1984, p.81.)

Chinese imperial seal of the Emperor Qianlong (1736-95). Ashmolean Museum, Oxford.

feature of the rebus, consequently, is that its apparent pictographic form does not necessarily correspond to its meaning.

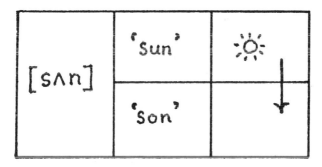

Fig. 1. A hypothetical English rebus. The problem of finding a symbol for the word 'son' is solved by borrowing the pictogram for the identically pronounced word 'sun'.

A rebus, then, is a secondary sign, in the sense that it presupposes the existence of a prior sign which supplies the link between its form and its meaning. This is also true, although in a rather different way, of the type of signs often called *determinatives*. These are supplementary signs used to clarify the intended interpretation of other signs. For example, if a script uses a circle with 'rays' as a pictogram to designate the word *sun*, and the pronunciation of this word is identical with that of *son* meaning 'male offspring', the two words might be distinguished in writing by representing the second as the circle pictogram followed by a pictogram of a human figure. This ancillary sign would be a determinative, indicating that the first pictogram should be interpreted not as *sun* but as *son*. Determinatives may also distinguish between alternative pronunciations of a sign. They are particularly common in alphabetic abbreviations. For instance, in 'Ch.' (standing for the name *Charles*), the second letter in effect functions as a determinative, distinguishing this use of the sign 'C' from its function as an initial of other names (*Christopher*, *Conrad*, etc.). Diacritics such as accent marks may also be regarded as a form of determinative: the presence or absence of an acute accent, for example, distinguishes the pronunciation of French *plie* ('plaice') from that of *plié* ('folded').

Actual usage of these terms is in various respects less straightforward than the above account might suggest. The term *pictogram* appears sometimes to be used to include almost any type of non-alphabetic symbol. Sometimes, on the other hand, pictograms are distinguished from ideograms by the criterion that the latter are 'abstract' signs (i.e. not recognisably pictorial). Most of the terminological confusion in this field may be attributed to three facts. The first is that many early texts remain undeciphered or only partially deciphered, with the consequence that the precise nature of the signs they employ is still a matter for speculation. The second is that there is no consensus among authorities as to how the various terms should be distinguished. The third is that a script may in general be characterised as, say, 'pictographic' or 'syllabic' when it is actually a mixture of signs of various types.

A further difficulty arising from the application of the terminology may be illustrated by reference to Egyptian hieroglyphs. According to Lurker,[6] hieroglyphs fall into three classes. One class (ideograms) comprises symbols which render a word without reference to its sound. Thus a rectangle with an opening below meant 'house'; two legs meant 'walk'; the lotus or reed, characteristic of Upper Egypt, meant 'south'; the conjoined signs for 'god' and 'servant' meant 'priest'; and the goose, the phonogram for 'son', together with the sun, stood for the king, as 'son of the sun'. A second class (phonograms) indicate either a consonant or a succession of two or three consonants. Vowels were not written. Thus the phonogram for 'goose' (*sz*) was also used to write the word for 'son', which had the same succession of consonants; and the phonogram for 'swallow' (*wr*) was used to write the word for 'great' (also *wr*). Hieroglyphs for words of one consonant could also be used as phonograms for that consonant. Thus the symbol for 'stool' (*p*) also stood for the consonant 'p', and the symbol for 'loaf' (*t*) also for the consonant 't'. The third class (determinatives) had no phonetic value but were placed at the end of a word to indicate its category. Thus the names of towns included the ideogram for 'town', and the word for 'locust' included the determinative symbol for 'goose', as representing flying creatures in general.

In Lurker's tri-partite classification – which in its own terms is clear enough – not only is the class of ideograms taken to subsume logograms and the class of phonograms to subsume rebuses, but the three classes are distinguished on functional criteria, with the result that the same sign can sometimes be classified in more than one way. Thus, for example, the goose sign is mentioned under all three heads: it is part of an ideogram for 'king', a phonogram for 'son', and a

---

[6] M. Lurker, *The Gods and Symbols of Ancient Egypt*, London, 1980, pp.62-4.

determinative for 'locust'. The only way to avoid this cross-classification would be to distinguish rigorously between a terminology of forms and a terminology of functions: but authorities on the history of writing on the whole fail to do this.

A further point to note is that the distinction between alphabetic and syllabic writing raises the question of how to classify systems of the kind found among Semitic scripts, which have signs for consonants only, and omit vowels altogether. It is sometimes argued that these are not alphabets and are better regarded as 'consonantal syllabaries', despite the fact that the term 'consonantal syllabary' seems in turn to be self-contradictory. More important than the resolution of this classificatory 'problem', however, is the significance of the way it is posed. The problem itself is generated by two assumptions. One is the assumption that a 'consonants only' system cannot be a 'true' alphabet, since the alphabets we are most familiar with are 'true' alphabets and they do indeed contain letters for vowels as well as letters for consonants. The other assumption is that a 'consonants only' system cannot be a 'true' syllabary either, since a 'true' syllabary is conceived of on the analogy of a 'true' alphabet and therefore must somehow accommodate vowels too. A 'consonants only' system is thus seen as neither one thing nor the other, a kind of graphological freak which does not conform to either of the two 'natural' alternatives for phonographic writing. This line of thinking fails altogether to take into account the fact that the practical utility of having separate signs for vowels will vary according to the phonological structure of the language concerned, just as will, for instance, the practical utility of having separate signs for voiced and voiceless consonants. What is viable as a writing system for one language is not necessarily viable for another, and the history of the alphabet amply illustrates this point. It is all the more ironical to find writing systems being classified and evaluated as if they should have been designed not to meet the practical needs of particular linguistic communities, but rather to serve the universal descriptive purposes of an Abstract Phonology.

More important still for our present purposes is the fact that the distinction between alphabetic and syllabic writing is drawn in such a way as to define the latter in terms of the former, thus reversing the actual historical sequence of development. This reversal already prejudges in various subtle ways a number of questions about the origin of writing. It is as if, retrospectively, evolution could be seen to have been gradually working towards the creation of an 'ideal' alphabet as its long-term goal.

Thus when one looks carefully at the traditional terminology used to discuss the history of writing, it becomes clear that the keystone of the whole conceptual structure is the alphabet. All the distinctions recognised are based directly or indirectly upon an initial opposition between alphabetic and non-alphabetic signs (Fig.2).[7] What this conceptual structure reflects, historically, is the ethnocentric bias of a European approach to non-European languages. In this sense, modern scholarship has unquestionably and unquestioningly taken the alphabet as its central paradigm example of a writing system. The consequences of this for the problem of the origin of writing are both far-reaching and distorting. They involve in one way or another some of the most basic assumptions underlying modern linguistic theory.

Fig. 2.

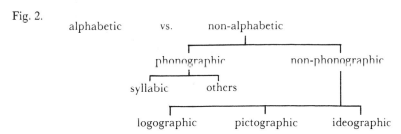

[7] A clear example is Pedersen's classification of writing systems. (H. Pedersen, *The Discovery of Language. Linguistic Science in the Nineteenth Century*, tr. J.W. Spargo, Bloomington, 1959, p.142.)

Unfortunately, the notion of an ideal alphabet holding up a mirror to phonetic reality is based on the assumption that in phonetic reality we find an antecedently given set of individual sounds. This assumption is called in question as soon as it is pointed out that it is equally possible to define individual sounds as, precisely, those complexes of acoustic features which are conventionally held to be represented by single letters of the alphabet. We might with no less justification choose to treat the syllable as the 'individual sound', and regard its consonantal and vocalic properties simply as constituent features of that individual sound. That syllables are 'larger' units than consonants or vowels proves nothing either way. For that matter, all consonant and vowel sounds may in turn be analysed systematically into 'smaller' phonetic components: it is perhaps merely a historical accident that no system of writing has ever adopted this alternative type of analysis as a basis for devising sets of signs. What at least is clear is that to assume straightaway that an English spoken word such as *bat* consists of just three 'individual sounds' because its written form comprises just three letters is simply to put the alphabetic cart before the phonetic horse. What needs first of all to be elucidated, here as in other cases, is what represents what.

Representation is a problem which recurs in various guises in twentieth-century theoretical linguistics. It has two complementary parts. On the one hand, there is the question of the relationship between a language and its 'representation' as portrayed in the descriptive linguist's account of its phonology, morphology, syntax, etc. On the other hand, there is the question of the relationship between this 'scientific' account and the 'representation' of the language in the minds of native speakers. So there is in fact a double problem of representation: but in both instances there can be no doubt that it was the alphabet which offered linguistic theorists their most readily available model of how the problem of representation might in principle be tackled. That is to say, ideally there would be a one-one correspondence between the representing symbols and the linguistic units or structures which they represented. An 'ideal' alphabet would exemplify this correspondence, at least as regards the pronunciation of the language. Analogous 'alphabets' at other linguistic levels can readily be constructed on this model. Correctness of representation is implicitly judged in terms of a correspondence of this 'alphabetic' type.

The ideal alphabet envisaged is thus one in which each letter would stand for just one individual sound, whether consonant or vowel, and there would be no redundant letters, no reduplication, and no need to represent any individual sound by a combination of letters. In short, the alphabet and the sound system would be mirror images of each other. In practice, alphabets generally employed for the recording of historical, legal and literary texts, in all cultures which have adopted alphabetic writing, fall short of this correspondence. The ideal, none the less, has exercised a profound influence upon the way in which laymen and scholars alike evaluate the use of alphabetic writing and treat some uses as 'better' or 'worse' or 'more rational' or 'less anomalous' than others.

By comparison with this alphabetic ideal, syllabic writing is automatically seen as something more primitive and clumsy. For syllabaries use symbols which fail to separate out the ultimate linear units of the sequence of sounds. They 'lump together' the consonant-vowel combinations which an ideal alphabet would represent individually. Less obvious, perhaps, is that even to say that a syllabary is a system of characters each of which stands either for a vowel or for some fixed combination of consonants and vowels is already to describe what a syllabary is in alphabetic terms. That is, the notion of consonants and vowels combining to form syllables of various kinds is itself an alphabetic notion. Once this perspective is adopted, it becomes extremely difficult to resist the implication that consonants and vowels are, in the nature of things, more basic elements than syllables, and hence syllabic writing somehow fails to come to terms with the real basis of speech, whereas alphabetic writing succeeds.

It is the same alphabetic bias which explains certain curious features of the way in which non-phonographic writing is analysed. For instance, it follows from the definitions given above that there is no reason why a pictogram should not also be an ideogram, and in fact such combinations are common in the modern international sign language of motorways and airports (the figure of a man indicating a toilet for men, the outline of a cup indicating the availability of beverages, etc.). It follows also that there are likely to be cases in which it is not clear whether to treat a sign as an ideogram or a logogram. (The dollar sign, it might be argued, functions as a substitute for the English word 'dollar' only in certain linguistic contexts, whereas in others it functions as a symbol standing for a certain national currency, independently of the name by which that currency happens to be designated in English.) In fact, the underlying rationale of the triple distinction between logogram, pictogram and ideogram is somewhat puzzling until we realise that what motivates these concepts, once again, is the implied contrast with alphabetic writing. Alphabetic writing typically does *not* (i) use word signs which give no indication of pronunciation, or (ii) use simplified pictures as characters, or (iii) represent ideas independently of any specific form of words. Thus logograms, pictograms and ideograms together represent, as it were, the negative side of a conceptualisation of writing which is dominated by the positive status assigned to the alphabet.

The alphabetic bias is, unfortunately, virtually endemic in Western education, where children are taught 'correct pronunciation' by being presented with alphabetic writing and required to 'read it aloud'. Their ability to do this is taken as an important indication of their progress towards 'literacy'. Saussure commented on the educational consequences of this practice in his *Cours de linguistique générale* as follows:

Grammarians are desperately eager to draw our attention to the written form. Psychologically, this is quite understandable, but the consequences are unfortunate. The use acquired by the words 'pronounce' and 'pronunciation' confirms this abuse and reverses the true relationship between writing and the language. Thus when people say that a certain letter should be pronounced in this way or that, it is the visual image which is mistaken for the model. If *oi* can be pronounced *wa*,[8] then it seems that *oi* must exist in its own right. Whereas the fact of the matter is that it is *wa* which is written *oi*. To explain this strange case, our attention is drawn to the fact that this is an exception to the usual pronunciation of *o* and *i*. But this explanation merely compounds the mistake, implying as it does that the language is subordinate to its spelling. The case is presented as contravening the spelling system, as if the orthographic sign were basic.[9]

The situation, however, is even worse than Saussure describes it. It is not simply a question of psychological perversion of the natural order of priorities between sounds and letters, but of something more fundamental. Saussure, whose phonetic theorising antedates the invention of the sound spectrograph, and also the modern systematisation of phonemic analysis, failed to realise to what extent his own basic assumption that speech comprises a linear sequence of discrete sounds was itself an extrapolation from the familiar structure of the written word. The notion that in speaking we select the individual consonants and vowels which somehow emerge from our mouths threaded in the right order like beads on a string is simply the image of alphabetic orthography projected back on to speech production.

One of the most striking examples of this in recent intellectual history is Wittgenstein's discussion of how it might be possible to train people as ideal 'reading machines' (*als Lesemaschinen*).[10] Central to this discussion is the notion

---

[8] As in the French word *roi* ('king'), pronounced [rwa].

[9] F. de Saussure, op. cit., p.30.

[10] *Philosophische Untersuchungen*, Oxford, 1953, § 157.

that what happens when we read aloud is that the eye scans a sequence of written characters and as a result the reader is 'guided' (by some process never clearly explained) to pronounce certain sounds. At one point in the discussion, Wittgenstein goes so far as to introduce a comparison with the operations of a pianola, where a mechanism is devised to ensure that certain notes are struck which correspond to holes in the surface of a revolving cylinder. Now no one would suppose Wittgenstein, of all philosophers, to be naive enough to equate the alphabet with a phonetic notation, or the human speaker with a machine which 'reads off' sounds from scripts in the manner of a pianola. Nevertheless, these are the ideas on which Wittgenstein's discussion is based. Where do they come from? Wittgenstein himself did not invent them: rather, he draws upon them as if such comparisons will be intuitively obvious to any intelligent person. And so perhaps they are. But only because they are founded upon a whole cultural tradition which has over the centuries built up an idealisation of what the alphabet would be if only it could.

Wittgenstein's description of the reading process, for all its philosophical subtlety, sounds like nothing so much as the description of a person suffering from a particular form of dyslexia. He appears to assume that reading is quite different from understanding the words one reads. It is simply a question of translating marks on a page into vocal equivalents, either aloud or 'in one's head', and nothing more. Now doubtless there are – perhaps rather rare – types of reading performance which would fit this description: a trained phonetician, for example, reading a phonetic transcript of a text in a language with which he is totally unfamiliar. But whether anything like that is a basic component of normal fluent reading is quite a different matter. The point here is that it is just such an image of what the reading process must essentially be that alphabetic writing itself projects; or, rather, of what it would be if the alphabet were an ideal phonetic notation.

Alphabetic tyranny of a no less insidious kind is indicated by the evidence which emerges from such a book as Iona and Peter Opie's *The Lore and Language of Schoolchildren.*[11] The alphabet provides an endless source of what the Opies call 'self-incrimination traps'. These are trick questions designed to induce the victim to say something stupid, vulgar, or otherwise reprehensible.[12] Typical are catches like 'Spell *olic* and say "stars" '; or 'Spell *I cup*'. The verbal mechanism of these spelling catches shows a number of interesting features. They are, as it were, childish versions of Bellerophon's deception. The catch is that the victim does not grasp – until it is too late – what the message he has been told to deliver actually means. But there is more to it than that. Often what the juvenile victim is asked to spell is not something which in the normal course of events would arise as orthographically problematic. The two examples just cited both illustrate this point. *Olic* is not an English word: at best it is a 'part' of words like *frolic, alcoholic* and *vitriolic*, all of which belong to a highly literate stratum of English vocabulary: so the chance of being asked to 'spell *olic*' in real life – even in real classroom life – are, to say the least, remote. Similarly, although there is an English verb *cup*, the number of occasions on which a schoolchild is likely to have encountered the paradigm *I cup, you cup, he cups, she cups,* etc. will not be high. Certainly by no means as high as the incidence of 'genuine' orthographic traps like 'How do you spell *friend*?' In short, the very existence of these joke questions which hinge on spelling tests of the most remote degree of plausibility points to the fact that modern education rapidly inculcates into children's minds the following principle: *anything I can say can be spelled*. For this is the basic premiss needed even to make sense of instructions like 'Spell *olic*' or 'Spell *I cup*'. These instructions, as employed in 'self-incrimination traps', do not need paper and pencil or

[11] Oxford, 1959.
[12] ibid., p.84ff.

blackboard and chalk. They are traps sprung orally in the playground, or on the way to school.

The significance of such games is not to be underestimated. We are already dealing, it would seem, with a culture in which even the youngest educational apprentices are deemed to be perfectly familiar with something which the Greek Stoic philosophers came to understand only after grappling with the problem for some time: that the elements of alphabetic writing can be identified in three ways, namely by sound, by shape and by name; the name being neither the name of the sound nor the name of the shape, but the name of a unit in a spelling system. Thus, as the popular children's counting-out formula puts it, 'O-U-T spells OUT': and it does so irrespective of whether the word thus spelled is written in capitals, in small letters, in italics or in gothic, and irrespective of how it happens to be pronounced. That is why the only correct oral answer to the instruction 'Spell *olic*' is to say the names of the letters: the trap might misfire if the victim could 'spell' simply by articulating the separate consonants and vowels, or by giving some other sequence of letters corresponding to that pronunciation e.g. *ollick*. Thus there is a folklore 'theory' of the alphabet already built into this classroom-cum-playground verb *to spell*. To ask how someone's name is spelled is not, in the light of this theory, either to ask how to pronounce it or to ask how to write it, even though the usual assumption is that one wants to know the spelling in order to be able to write it. Nevertheless, a child not yet able to read or write its own name may well know how to spell it, in this sense of the verb. Although correct spelling is normally manifest in correct writing, the dependence is the other way round, at least according to the folklore theory: that is, the written forms are correctly written only if they are correctly spelled. Thus for *homo alphabeticus* spelling comes to take priority both over speech and over writing: it establishes a level of linguistic articulation more basic than either. To be able to pronounce a word but not know how to spell it is treated as just as much a sign of ignorance as to write it wrongly spelled.

Perhaps the most striking testimony of all to the tyranny of the alphabet is the fact that the first European to study the language of the Maya Indians, the Franciscan Diego de Landa in the sixteenth century, seems to have been convinced that Maya hieroglyphs were a form of alphabetic writing. He produced, with the help of informants, a Maya alphabet of 27 characters, which scholars later tried to use without success in deciphering Maya inscriptions. It appears that what he must have done was to ask his informants how they wrote the names of the Spanish letters, and his informants wrote down the hieroglyphic symbol for what they took to be his mispronunciation of native Maya words. So Landa's Maya alphabet stands as a kind of permanent folly in the history of linguistics. What it reveals is the depths of incomprehension which centuries of alphabetic culture can inculcate about the nature of writing.

Fig. 3. Landa's Maya 'alphabet'. (*Relación de las Cosas de Yucatán*, ed. H.P. Martinez, Mexico, 1938, p.208.)

The tyranny of the alphabet is part of that scriptist bias which is deeply rooted in European education.[13] It fosters respect for the written word over the spoken, and respect for the book above all as a repository of both the language and the wisdom of former ages. At first sight, the insistence that writing is only a representation of speech may appear to run quite counter to the prevailing scriptism of European culture. But that appearance is deceptive. The doctrine that writing represents speech becomes a cornerstone of scriptism once the written representation is held to be not a slavish or imperfect copy but, on the contrary, an idealisation which captures those essential features often blurred or distorted in the rough and tumble of everyday utterance. Thus it is possible for the written representation to be held up as a model of what the spoken reality ought to be.

The fact is that writing and speech in Western civilisation have for centuries been locked in a relationship which is essentially symbiotic. So close has this relationship been that it is difficult to prise the two apart. The Greeks did not distinguish consistently between speech-sounds and letters; and two thousand years later Saussure could still accuse one of the most distinguished philologists of the nineteenth century of confusing languages with alphabets.[14]

Ironically, it is the price we pay for making the effort to disentangle speech from writing that each is then defined by reference to the other. Speech is thought of in terms of the pronunciation of written forms. Writing is thought of as a way of setting down speech. These complementary oversimplifications have been long established in many areas of education. They have been profoundly influential in shaping the form taken by linguistic theory itself.

This is in part attributable to the fact that although it is easy enough to see where the oversimplification lies, it is far from

[13] R. Harris, *The Language-Makers*, London, 1980, p.6ff.
[14] F. de Saussure, op.cit., p.46.

easy to avoid it. For most purposes it is plausible to suppose it does not matter anyway: it suffices simply to 'bear in mind' that we are dealing with an oversimplification. Not for all purposes, however. If we are concerned with securing a firm conceptual grasp of the basic mechanisms of language, then it will not do to bow to the expediencies of oversimplification and leave it at that. What writing is must count as a question which lies at the heart of linguistics (although it is a question more often dismissed than addressed by contemporary linguistic theorists). To acknowledge the oversimplification leads immediately to the horrendous problem of proposing an alternative account of the relationship.

The depths of difficulty involved may be illustrated even from as simple a matter as explaining the difference between the two following examples:

(i) I love to see, when leaves depart, the clear anatomy arrive, winter, the paragon of art, that kills all forms of life and feeling save what is pure and will survive.

(ii) I love to see, when leaves depart,
The clear anatomy arrive,
Winter, the paragon of art,
That kills all forms of life and feeling
Save what is pure and will survive.[15]

An initial move might be to say that the first example is written as prose and the second as verse. But is the distinction between prose and verse itself a distinction of speech or of writing? The moment we say it belongs to both, we are back with that original symbiosis which left us uncertain how to distinguish the two. Perhaps it will be claimed that the convention of arranging lines neatly on a page one below another, as distinct from the rambling continuity of prose, together with accompanying difference in the use of capital

[15] Roy Campbell, *Collected Poems*, London, 1949, p.52.

letters, are clearly conventions of writing. But is it so clear? Is it not, rather, the rhythm and the rhyme of the spoken verse to which we must appeal in order to make any sense of such conventions? And if that is so, can we say that these are conventions of writing as such? The attempt to prise speech and writing apart opens up one gap here only to close another there.

Those addicted to the fashionable reduction of linguistic questions to the formulation of 'rules' will doubtless not be slow to point out that, at least as far as English is concerned, although it is relatively easy to devise a set of 'rules' for rewriting examples of type (ii) as examples of type (i), it is remarkably difficult (if not impossible) to do the reverse. That is to say, given a sample of English verse, it can be 'rewritten' as prose with few or no exceptions to a list of general instructions, which have to do with matters like capitalisation after a comma, beginning new lines, and so on. Whereas, given a sample of English prose, we have no guarantee at all that any set of rules is available which will rewrite it into a canonical English verse form traditionally acknowledged. It is impossible to make octosyllabic couplets out of the Gettysburg address, at least as it stands, or stood. But had the Gettysburg address been couched in octosyllabic couplets in the first place, there would have been no difficulty about re-writing them as English prose, either then or now. One point of this example is to focus upon the sense which the term *writing* acquires when we relate it to its modern technical or quasi-technical derivative *rewriting*. A more general and more important question, however, concerns what this asymmetry of conversion between prose and verse forms tells us about the distinction between writing and speech. For it is far from clear that in speech *as such* the asymmetry has any counterpart at all. Can anyone now 'respeak' the Gettysburg address (as distinct from reading Lincoln's words aloud, or rephrasing his message)? Thinking about that difficulty may lead us to see in what respects questions of linguistic theory are still – as ever –

at the mercy of the usage and etymology of the terms in which they are couched.

Perhaps some will feel tempted to argue that the distinction between prose and verse is in the final analysis a distinction of speech, because the sentence of the first example would be read differently from the sentence of the second, although the words in both cases are the same. Certainly it would seem possible – at least, in many instances – to distinguish audibly between words read 'as prose' and the same words read 'as verse'. But the problem thus settled immediately bobs up again, behind our backs this time. For how can we establish that the very distinction between a prose-reading voice and a verse-reading voice is not itself a reflection of a prior distinction in writing? What tells the reader to read in one voice rather than another is, arguably, the disposition of written forms seen on the page.

Then again, is it true to say that in the two cases the words *are* the same? Or if we insist that they are, are we not then insisting precisely on that equation between spoken and written units which is part of the question at issue? One of the ever-present pitfalls in arguments about the distinction between writing and speech is that the modern relationship between the two is such as to facilitate and even encourage circularity of this kind. Whether we refer here to the 'same words', 'same phrases', or 'same sentences', the postulated sameness cannot ultimately free itself from that symbiotic interlocking between speech and writing which gave us the basis for comparison in the first place.

Least of all does it help if we invoke the fact that poetic traditions flourish even in pre-literate societies. That does not prove that the distinction between prose and verse must ultimately be independent of writing altogether. For it begs the question of what happens to poetry once it becomes written. We cannot take it for granted that awareness of spelling, or knowledge of manuscript and typographic conventions, play no part in the literate poet's processes of creative composition. On the contrary, it begins to make less and less sense to ask whether the literate poet composed the poem 'aloud' and then wrote it down; or composed the poem 'on paper' and then recited it to find out what it sounded like. This would be to confuse the hammers and nails of composition with the workmanship itself. One might as well ask whether Beethoven strummed a few notes absent-mindedly on the piano before it occurred to him that this sounded like a good tune; or whether he wrote down a random configuration of blobs on stave lines and wondered what the result would be if he played them.

What seems at least uncontentious is that the opening stanza of Roy Campbell's poem is both 'readable' and 'readable aloud'. But that is not an intrinsic characteristic of written poetry, nor of writing. For there are conventions of writing available to the literate poet which do not need the backing of any spoken correlate. There are, in other words, 'unspeakable' poems. One example, also on the subject of life, death and survival, is Robert Richardson's *Nuclear Breathing Exercises* (see opposite).

The claim that some of these lines can be read, but not read aloud, may need preliminary clarification. Certainly they can all be rendered in some audible form or other, if anyone insists. But this will in the end come down to expedients like saying the names of individual letters: and that is not, in the relevant sense, reading aloud. No one when asked to 'read aloud' a sonnet by Shakespeare starts spelling out the first word. True, Robert Richardson is not William Shakespeare: but it makes no difference in this instance. For it would defeat the purpose of Richardson's poem to insist on a full oral version of it, just as it would defeat the purpose of Shakespeare's to start spelling it out. The poetic point of this breakdown in the mechanism of reading aloud is closely connected with the physiological act of breathing. The poem breathes its last on what traditional grammar calls a final consonant. But a consonant, according to the etymological definition, requires other phonetic elements to accompany it in order to be

```
BREATHE  IN
BREATHE  OUT
BREATHE  IN
BREATHE  OUT
BREATHE  IN
BREATHE  OUT
BREATHE  IN
 REATHE  OUT
BREAT    IN
    EATHE OUT
BREA     IN
     ATHE OUT
BRE      IN
     THE  OUT
BR       IN
      HE OUT
B        IN
       E OUT
         IN
         OUT
       I
         UT

       T
```

pronounced: and here none are left. That isolated final consonant is the final self-contradiction of nuclear phonetics.

No simple-minded account of writing as a mere transcription of speech affords the least insight into the techniques of poetic composition here. It is in the end irrelevant how a final *t* might or might not be pronounced in English. What is relevant is that it is read orthographically as the final letter of *out*: the last exit.

Thinking through such problems should bring us quite quickly to realise that there is no facile distinction to be made between writing-as-visible-marks, on the one hand, as opposed to speech-as-audible-sounds on the other. For it is of the essence of full literacy of the modern sophisticated kind that it entails the integration in consciousness of speech with writing. Marks on a page are no more the poem than sound waves are:

which is to say that speech is also more than the latter, just as writing is more than the former.

What such examples as these point to may seem to make the question of the origin of writing initially even more puzzling. In one sense that is all to the good, because that question itself has had its true intellectual content emasculated by those aforementioned oversimplifications about the relationship between writing and speech. Once we grant, however hesitantly, that it is just as naive to assume that writing is merely speech fixed on a surface as it is to assume that speech is writing ephemerally liberated into thin air, at least the way is open to a less prejudiced inquiry into the place writing occupies in the complex of human abilities and activities we now call 'language'.

Every question takes on a different significance as we put it in a different context. The question of the origin of writing is no exception. In one context, the strategy for answering it may seem so obvious to any person capable of reading that it is hardly worth serious discussion. Since we already know what writing is, we merely trace back that practice called 'writing' until we discover when and where it starts. The very simplicity of the problem disguises its complexity, as with almost all inquiries into cultural practices worth undertaking. As regards 'What is writing?', the sole difficulty might seem to be framing an answer of sufficient generality to encompass the enormous diversity of the world's known writing systems. It would need to be an answer which applied equally to specimens of writing as diverse as, for example, Egyptian hieroglyphs, Japanese hiragana and modern English. But framing an answer to cope with such problems surely cannot be beyond the wit of man. Robust confidence of this order already puts the question in an academic context which invites confusion between the origin of writing and the genesis of scripts.

The question of the origin of writing might seem almost sacrilegious if we lived in a society where *writing*, or a translational equivalent of that term, were the name of some graphic mystery known only to high priests and performed in the inmost of tabernacles on holy occasions. It might seem, on the other hand, utterly trivial if we lived in a society which restricted the term *writing* to the exercise of one specific technique, and did not apply it also to the products of that technique. As it is, ours is a society familiar with uses of the term *writing* which license its application to a whole range of arts, crafts, skills and products, ranging from calligraphy to the composition of musical scores and television scripts. The very multiplicity of these applications itself marks out a certain form of civilisation.

In posing the question of the origin of writing, then, we cannot expect to be able to shrug off effortlessly the many implications of the fact that the Western tradition itself is a tradition founded on literacy. We cannot ignore, for example, the fact that language studies within that tradition have always been based on the implicit and unquestioned assumption that there is a 'special relationship' between writing and speech which allows what is spoken to be reduced to writing and thus handed on from one generation to the next. But exactly what form that 'special relationship' takes and how far back it goes in human history are issues which immediately become open to question once we ask for an account of the origin of writing. For we have no warrant to project back indefinitely into prehistory a conceptualisation of writing which is itself the product of the uses of literacy in a highly sophisticated civilisation.

If the problem of the origin of writing is to be put in its proper historical perspective, we need to begin by setting aside, if we can, the whole of this deeply rooted tangle of scriptist preconceptions about the relationship between writing and speech. To see why this is essential, it will be useful to examine next how such preconceptions render 'evolutionary' accounts of the origin of writing explanatorily sterile.

Even for this limited purpose, however, it will be necessary to fix on certain interpretations of terms which relate to the

Juxtaposed pictorial and scriptorial signs. The death of King Harold as recorded on the Bayeux tapestry.

Syntactically integrated pictorial and scriptorial signs.

distinctions one needs to draw. An obvious distinction
(however it is ultimately to be defined) will be between the
kinds of things Tarzan called 'bugs' in his primer and the
kinds of things he counted as illustrations. In the following
discussion, it will be convenient to designate the latter *pictorial*
signs and the former *scriptorial* signs. Where the boundary
between pictorial and scriptorial signs falls will patently be one
of the contentious issues to be resolved. Consequently, it will
also be necessary to have a term which is neutral with respect
to that particular distinction; and for this purpose it is proposed
to adopt the term *graphic* sign as referring to pictorial signs,
scriptorial signs, or both. Which graphic signs are pictorial and
which are scriptorial is in many cases not a problem. For
example, we have no doubt that the Bayeux tapestry gives us

both a pictorial record of certain historical events and also, accompanying that pictorial record – or, more exactly, visually superimposed upon it – a sequence of scriptorial signs in the form of explanatory sentences written in Latin. Likewise, we have no doubt that a road sign combines, say, the pictorial sign of a motor car together with the scriptorial message 'Except for access'. It may be altogether less obvious, however, in many cases. Finally, since we do not wish to pre-judge the questions of whether or to what extent a pictorial sign always bears a recognisable visual resemblance to what it stands for, it will be useful to reserve the terms *iconic* and *iconicity* for that visual relationship. This will leave us free to allow that a pictorial sign is not necessarily iconic, or that the degree of its iconicity may be open to doubt.

Chapter Three

The Evolutionary Fallacy

That Writing, in the earliest ages of the world, was a delineation of the outlines of those things men wanted to remember, rudely graven either upon shells or stones, or marked upon the leaves or bark of trees; and that this simple representation of forms was next succeeded by symbolic figures, will generally be allowed.

Charles Davy, 1772

If the alphabet is tacitly accepted as the paradigm case of a writing system, and if the alphabet itself is known to have evolved from earlier phonographic writing systems, then the most promising area to search for the origin of writing itself would seem to be the area occupied by the most primitive phonographic systems and their predecessors. We are automatically led in this way to look for some kind of 'evolutionary' solution to the problem.

It is not surprising, therefore, to find that historians of the development of writing systems often distinguish between 'true' writing and its precursors. Cohen speaks of 'protowriting' (*protoécriture*).[1] Février envisages a transition from 'synthetic' to 'analytic' writing.[2] Gelb distinguishes between 'full writing' and primitive 'semasiography'.[3] On what criteria are such distinctions based?

Cohen identifies protowriting with pictography and denies

---

[1] M. Cohen, *La grande invention de l'écriture et son évolution*, Paris, 1958, p.27ff.

[2] J.G. Février, *Histoire de l'écriture*, Paris, 1948, p.10.

[3] I.J. Gelb, op.cit., p.190ff.

that pictography is true writing, on the grounds that it gives no detailed representation of spoken discourse and is independent of any particular language. He distinguishes between pictogram-signs and pictogram-signals. The former are used to convey a message directly to the recipient by visual means (thus a drawing of a bird may function as a pictogram-sign for a bird). The latter are simply mnemonic devices which assist in recalling a verbal message and cannot be 'read' unless the message is already known to the 'reader'. (Thus a drawing of a bird may function as a pictogram-signal for the proverb 'A bird in the hand is worth two in the bush'.) For Cohen, the essential stage in the transition from pictography to true writing is the use of pictogram-signs as rebuses. A rebus utilises the pictogram-sign corresponding to a certain word in order to represent the pronunciation of another word or the pronunciation of part of another word. Thus a pictogram of a bee might be used as a rebus to stand for the English verb *be* or for the first syllable of the word *belief*. A complete rebus representation of the word *belief* might use the pictogram of a bee followed by the pictogram of a leaf. On Cohen's view, certain systems may occupy an intermediary position between pictography and 'true' writing. An example of such a system for Cohen is Aztec. In Aztec, for instance, the particle *tlan* 'in, among' is represented by a pictogram of teeth, the word for 'teeth' being *tlantli*. But recourse to the rebus never became systematised in Aztec: it was used only in cases where purely pictographic representation was impossible for lack of a perspicuous visual image. None the less, Cohen grants Aztec the status of writing insofar as and because, if only haphazardly, it employs the rebus principle.

A broadly similar position is taken by Gelb. Gelb identifies semasiography as the 'forerunner of writing', and distinguishes within semasiography between 'descriptive-representational' devices and 'identifying-mnemonic' devices. This corresponds partially, although not exactly, to Cohen's distinction between pictogram-signs and pictogram-signals.

Gelb cites as an example of 'descriptive-representational' semasiography a letter sent by a Southern Cheyenne Indian to his son at the Pine Ridge Agency, Dakota. The letter is simply a line drawing which shows two Indians facing each other. Above the head of one are two turtles, and above the head of the other a small homunculus figure. From the mouth of the former Indian emerge lines which connect with a second homunculus, partially hidden behind the second Indian. Between and above the two Indians are a number of small round objects. The letter was understood by its recipient as saying that his father wished him to come and see him, and was arranging for the sum of 53 dollars to be placed to his son's credit in order to defray the expenses of the journey. The

Fig. 4. Cheyenne Indian letter from Turtle-Following-His-Wife to Little-Man. (G. Mallery, *Picture-Writing of the American Indians*, Washington, 1893, p.364.)

explanation of the drawing is that the father's name is 'Turtle-Following-His Wife', the son's name is 'Little Man', and the small round objects, fifty-three in number, are dollar coins. 'Identifying-mnemonic' devices, on the other hand, are typified for Gelb by potters' and masons' marks which identify the maker by means of an arbitrarily chosen symbol which has no connexion at all with his name. Thus potter Peter may choose to impress on the pots he makes a five-pointed star, simply because the design of a five-pointed star appeals to him, and no other potter has adopted it as his mark, but not because there is any other connexion at all between the star and the name *Peter*.

According to Gelb, it is the 'identifying-mnemonic' device, rather than the 'descriptive-representational' device which 'lies on the direct road toward a fully developed writing'.[4] This is because the former establishes a completely conventionalised correspondence between the symbol and what the symbol represents. Since what the symbol represents will have a name in the spoken language, this connexion establishes a further correspondence between the symbol and the spoken word. This leads naturally in the direction of a system of 'logography', or word signs. In Gelb's opinion no complete logographic system was ever developed, because it would have been impractically cumbersome to devise logographs for every word in a language. Instead, the crucial step towards 'full writing' was taken by the phonetisation implicit in rebus representation. Systematic phonetisation made possible 'the expression of any linguistic form by means of symbols with conventional syllabic values'.[5] Thus 'full' writing originated. Full writing, for Gelb, is 'phonography', as distinct from semasiography.

A distinction between 'real writing' and 'picture writing' is drawn somewhat differently by Bloomfield.[6] Bloomfield cites,

[4] ibid., p.192.
[5] ibid., p.194.
[6] L. Bloomfield, op.cit., p.282ff.

as examples of picture writing, types which correspond to Gelb's 'descriptive-representational' and 'identifying-mnemonic'. One example of the former is a picture sent to a fur trader by a Mandan Indian. In the centre are two crossed lines, on one side of which are drawings of a gun and of a beaver with twenty-nine parallel strokes above the beaver, while on the other side are drawings of a fisher, an otter and a buffalo. The interpretation is: 'I am ready to trade a fisher-skin, an otter-skin, and a buffalo-hide for a gun and thirty beaver-pelts.' Bloomfield's example of the 'identifying-mnemonic' type is a strip of birch bark on which an Ojibwa Indian had carved a series of pictures to remind himself of the succession of verses in a sacred song.

For Bloomfield, *picture-writing* is a 'misleading' term, since although what is called picture writing has the communicational advantages of permanence and transportability, it falls short of writing in bearing 'no fixed relation to linguistic forms'. 'Real writing', by contrast, is distinguished by two criteria. One is that the characters employed represent linguistic elements of some kind, and the other is that the characters employed to do this are limited in number. A 'character' Bloomfield defines as 'a uniform mark or set of marks which people produce under certain conditions and to which, accordingly, they respond in a certain way'.[7]

Bloomfield also objects to the term *ideographic* as applied to systems of writing which use one symbol for each word. He proposes to replace it by *logographic*. 'The important thing about writing,' he says, 'is precisely this, that the characters represent not features of the practical world ("ideas"), but features of the writers' language.'[8] The main difficulty with logographic writing, Bloomfield notes, is providing symbols 'for words whose meaning does not lend itself to pictorial representation'. He regards the rebus as 'the most important

[7] ibid., p.284.
[8] ibid., p.285.

device of this sort' and cites among other examples the ancient Egyptian use of the character depicting a conventionalised checkerboard not only for the word *mn* meaning 'checkers' but also for the homonymous verb *mn* meaning 'remain', and a double checkerboard for the verb *mnmn* 'move'. 'In the device of representing unpicturable words by phonetically similar picturable words,' he observes, 'we see the emergence of the phonetic factor in writing.'[9] The symbols become phonograms, rather than logograms, and this leads to the development of syllabaries, in which each character has a fixed syllabic value.

Février identifies 'synthetic' writing as 'writing of ideas' (*Ideenschrift*), as distinct from 'analytic' writing, which is 'ideographic', or 'writing of words' (*Wortschrift*).[10] Both these stages are prior to 'phonetic' writing, in which written characters designate sounds only. The crucial difference between the synthetic and analytic stages, according to Février, is that analytic writing is no longer 'arbitrary'. That is to say, it no longer allows the intervention of individual ingenuity or idiosyncrasy in devising or interpreting graphic signs. It establishes 'un stock de signes à valeur constante', since the value of each sign is identified with a word in the (spoken) language. An important transition preceding even the synthetic stage is the development of the use of pictorial images as mnemonic devices from their primitive use as magic symbols.[11] Finally, the use of the rebus to supplement the inadequacies of pictography at the synthetic stage 'leads almost inevitably' to phonetic writing.[12]

Diringer distinguishes between 'embryo-writing' and 'writing proper' or 'true writing'. Embryo-writing includes both 'mnemonic' and 'symbolic' signs. Within true writing, he

[9] ibid., p.287.
[10] Février, op.cit., p.10.
[11] ibid., p.32ff.
[12] ibid., p.107.

draws further distinctions. For Diringer, writing 'literally and closely defined' is 'the graphic counterpart of speech, the fixing of spoken language in a permanent or semi-permanent form'.[13] Writing thus 'presupposes the existence of spoken language': that is to say, the relationship between the two is a matter of definition, not a mere fact of historical antecedence. Embryo-writings, as opposed to true writing, are simply schematic figures of animals, geometric patterns, crude pictures of objects and scenes of various kinds, all scratched, drawn or painted by primitive peoples, and dating in the earliest known instances from the Upper Paleolithic period. Embryo-writings are intrinsically 'static': although capable of expressing quite vividly single, disconnected events or images, they are incapable of combining these into a sequence or discourse of any kind.

Diringer recognises five categories of 'true writing'. (i) The most rudimentary is that of 'pictography', which Diringer equates with 'picture writing'. It is distinguished from embryo-writing by not being restricted to the recording of 'single, disconnected images'. It can represent 'simple narrative' by means of a sequence of pictograms. However it lacks 'intrinsic phonetism' and can be 'expressed orally in any language without alteration of content'.[14] (ii) The second category of 'true writing' is 'ideographic' writing. This marks an advance over pictography in that the signs used, in addition to representing things, may 'connote as well the underlying ideas or conceptions with which those things are bound up'.[15] Thus a circle, which in pictography might represent the sun, might in ideographic writing also stand for heat, light, a god associated with the sun, or the word 'day'. But in ideographic, as in pictographic writing, the signs 'can be read with equal facility in any language'. (iii) The third category comprises

[13] D. Diringer, *Writing*, London, 1962, p. 13.
[14] ibid., p.21.
[15] ibid., p.22.

'analytic transitional scripts'. These are not purely ideographic, but introduce phonetic elements as well. Thus they stand somewhere in between 'pure ideographic' and 'pure phonetic' writing. The term 'analytic' here implies that the basic unit which the script represents is the word. (iv) The fourth category comprises 'phonetic scripts', in which we have 'for the first time, the graphic counterpart of speech', each element in such a script corresponding to 'a sound or sounds in the language which is being represented'.[16] (v) The fifth category is that subdivision of phonetic scripts comprising alphabetic writing, in which the signs represent 'single sounds', as distinct from syllables or combinations of sounds.

What Diringer calls the 'prototypal development of a script' is a development from embryo-writing through pictography to ideography, and then to phonetic writing of some kind. This transition to phonetic writing is commonly made via the use of certain signs as rebuses. In certain cases, however, the 'prototypal' sequence may not be followed. Diringer cites Sumerian as an example of a development which skips the purely ideographic stage and evolves straight from pictography to an analytic transitional script.

In spite of differences of detail and terminology, there is an unmistakable family resemblance between the accounts summarised above, and all are unsatisfactory in related respects. First, one wonders why a distinction should be drawn between two types of 'pre-writing' on the basis of mnemonic vs. representational function. The two categories in practice overlap. For example, one of the mnemonic symbols on the bark strip used by Bloomfield's Ojibwa Indian is the figure of a fox: but the reason for adopting this symbol was that a fox was mentioned in the verse of the song which this symbol 'represented'.[17]

Worse still, the examples which the authorities cite as representative of one of their two categories sometimes seem

[16] ibid., p.23.
[17] Bloomfield, op.cit., p.283.

better suited to exemplify the other. Thus Gelb's example of the letter from the Southern Cheyenne Indian to his son is baffling as an illustration of 'descriptive-representational' semasiography. For, as Métraux[18] points out, only someone who already knows the expression 'Turtle-Following-His-Wife' (*and knows that it is an Indian personal name*) is likely to be able to make sense of the drawing which shows an Indian with two turtles above his head. It is an 'identifying-mnemonic' rather than a 'descriptive-representational'device. Furthermore, unless it is recognised for what it is, the rest of the 'letter' makes no sense either. For there is nothing in the drawing to indicate that the two turtles fulfil a quite different semiotic function from, say, the fifty-three small round objects. In short, although a distinction between 'descriptive-representational' and 'identifying-mnemonic' devices may in abstract terms be clear enough, in practice it is difficult to separate one from the other because pictography relies so heavily upon the interpreter's presumed acquaintance with the circumstances of the message.

More generally, contrasting 'mnemonic-identificational' with 'descriptive-representational' devices seems to set up a quite artificial opposition between criteria relating to purpose and criteria relating to design. In one sense, all symbolic communication must involve mnemonic devices, since the symbols remind their interpreter of certain things connected with them by prior association, and are produced precisely for this purpose. But equally, all symbolic communication must involve 'representational' devices, in the sense that a symbol presupposes an interpretation which connects its form with a meaning of some kind. The crucial question is how to construe the notion of 'representation' in this context.

A pictogram consisting simply of a circle no more represents the sun than it represents the moon, or a football, or the

[18] A. Métraux, 'Les primitifs. Signaux et symboles. Pictogrammes et protoécriture', *L'écriture et la psychologie des peuples*, Paris, 1963, p.11.

fifteenth letter of the English alphabet – except within the context of a particular representational convention. But how about a pictogram of a bee? Does not a pictogram of a bee represent – first and foremost, at least – a bee, regardless of what else it may secondarily represent? The pass is sold once the question is put in this form. What first requires explanation is the descriptive expression 'pictogram of a bee'. For that description has a built-in 'representational' interpretation of the symbol. But it is not difficult to invent sign systems in which the 'bee' symbol stands for honey, sweetness, flattery, the month of July, or anything else *except* a bee. So the answer once again is that a pictogram 'of a bee' no more represents a bee than it represents honey, sweetness, etc., except within the context of a particular representational convention. Any claim to the contrary must ultimately rest upon an extremely controversial premiss, which is that certain forms of representation are natural and ineluctable, whereas others are not. (This, as it happens, is precisely the thesis underlying the argument about language in Plato's *Cratylus* and it is an issue which will come up for discussion again later.)

One cannot look at the distinction which theorists have drawn between their two primitive types of 'pre-writing' without at least entertaining the suspicion that elaborating that apparently unhelpful distinction in the first place will later on enable them to put across a point which would otherwise appear unconvincing. And indeed that is how it turns out. For a pivotal position in their account of the evolution of writing is always occupied by the rebus. Now the peculiar property of the rebus is that it apparently combines the 'mnemonic' and 'representational' functions of symbols in a special way. It simultaneously 'represents' one word and 'reminds' you of another. The 'reminder' is based on purely formal resemblance or identity: the pictogram of a bee represents a bee but also reminds you of the verb *be*, because the words happen to be phonologically indistinguishable in English.

Ingenious as the rebus theory is, it does not stand up to scrutiny. Linguists find it attractive because they are nowadays committed to the principle that the linguistic sign is arbitrary: and what could be more arbitrary than the identical phonological realisation of such semantically different words as *bee* and *be*? The rebus does indeed exemplify admirably this principle of arbitrariness. But what is unconvincing is the claim that it provides a bridge from logographic representation to phonographic representation. Using the pictogram of a bee to write the verb *be* does not in itself constitute an innovatory attempt to represent pronunciation. On the contrary, it reaffirms the logographic method, by allowing one word to borrow another word's symbol. The fact that as a result two words identically pronounced share the same symbol does not mean that the symbol now stands for a pronunciation rather than for the words in question. It simply means that the symbol has now acquired a new meaning in addition to the one which originally motivated the pictogram.

To treat the use of the rebus as the beginning of phonography is just as questionable as to suppose that representing the name *Stephen* by a picture of a step followed by a picture of a hen might constitute an initial move towards the pictorial analysis of orthography. The boot in both cases is on the wrong foot. What validates the step-and-hen picture-strip is indeed the recognition that the nouns *step* and *hen* present the same sequence of letters as the name *Stephen*. But that does not somehow turn pictures of steps or hens into pictorial representations of letter sequences, or even embryonic attempts at such representations. The reason why is obvious. The rebus is based on random identities of form. It affords no basis for systematisation of any kind; and that is precisely what is required in order to produce a method of representing pronunciations or spellings as such. Given any rebus (or even any set of rebuses) for the verb *be*, for example, one cannot extrapolate a general rule which allows one to proceed to construct the uniquely appropriate graphic for *beam, bean, beak,* etc. Why not? Because the association which gave rise to the original rebus was fortuitous in the first place. What is required to bring *be, beam, bean, beak,* etc. under the same

The Narmer palette, obverse. Egyptian Museum, Cairo.

system of formal representation is not an extension of the rebus principle but a complete break with it. The rebus was never the beginning of phonography but merely the dead end of logography.

The place of honour accorded to the rebus by historians of writing simply reflects their own prior assumption that 'progress' in the evolution which led ultimately to the alphabet must have consisted in developing systems which reflected more fully the structure of the spoken language. This is entirely in accord with the Aristotelian doctrine that writing is just a representation of speech. By comparison with simple logography, therefore, the rebus is seen as marking an

The Narmer palette, reverse. Egyptian Museum, Cairo.

'advance'. For the rebus principle reflects the structure of the spoken language more faithfully than the logographic principle, inasmuch as the rebus is based upon the recognition of homonyms in speech.[19]

A different evolutionary account from any so far mentioned

[19] The rebus is in certain instances even promoted to occupying the initial stage in the development of a script. For example, the early Egyptian slate tablet from Hierakonpolis known as the 'Narmer palette' (*c.* 3000 B.C.) is sometimes alleged to show the transition from pictorial recording to hieroglyphs. According to Gelb, the palette includes examples of rebus-writing to render proper names (notably the name 'Nar-mer', otherwise unknown in Egyptology, but identified by some scholars with Menes, founder of the First Dynasty).

Clay tokens from Susa, *c.* 3000 B.C. Musée du Louvre, Paris.

is proposed by Schmandt-Besserat,[20] who rejects the theory that the earliest form of writing was pictographic. Writing developed, according to Schmandt-Besserat, out of the primitive accounting system used in Mesopotamia from the ninth millennium B.C. onwards. This system was based on clay tokens or counters of various geometrical shapes, spheres, discs, cones, tetrahedrons, etc. The tokens were used originally to keep records of flocks, herds, and agricultural produce, each token standing for one animal or one unit and the different shapes distinguishing (arbitrarily) between the different species of animals (sheep, cows, etc.) or products (grain, oil, wool, etc.). Such tokens have been found in plenty at archaeological sites scattered over a wide area from south-western Turkey to Pakistan. Perhaps the earliest come from Tepe Asiab and Ganj-i-Dareh Tepe in Iran.

This accounting system, according to the theory, would have been necessitated by the development of an agricultural economy based on animal rearing and crops. In the earliest phase, the system could have managed with tokens of a very limited number of shapes. Any increase in the classes of item to be inventoried would be accommodated either by introducing a new shape, or by modifying one of the existing types in some distinctive way, thus creating a 'subtype'. The tokens found at Tepe Asiab and Ganj-i-Dareh Tepe, dating from about 8500 B.C., have been classified as falling into not more than twenty types and subtypes, the subtypes including semi-spheres and cones, spheres and disks bearing various incisions and punch marks. Excavations at a neighbouring site, Tepe Sarab, uncovered tokens dating from about 6500 B.C. which showed twenty-eight types and subtypes. This very small increase in the number of distinctive tokens over a period of some two thousand years is taken to indicate that both the economy and its accounting system remained very stable in its primitive phase for a long time.

[20] D. Schmandt-Besserat, 'The earliest precursor of writing', *Scientific American*, Vol.238 No. 6, June 1978, pp.38-47.

This situation began to change, however, in the fourth millennium B.C. with the rise of cities, where large populations lived by specialising in various trades and crafts, including the making of bronze, stone and pottery artifacts. The development of this new urban economy would have placed an unprecedented strain on the traditional accounting system, since the classes of items to be inventoried were many more than under the earlier agricultural economy. The result can be seen in the great proliferation in the variety of tokens found at late-fourth-millennium sites such as Uruk, Tello and Fara in Iraq, Susa and Chogha Mish in Iran, and Habuba Kabira in Syria. The tokens appear in new geometrical shapes, including parabolas and rhomboids, and there is a great increase in the number of subtypes distinguished by incisions of various kinds and added pellets or coils of clay. Altogether some 15 types and 250 subtypes have been dated to this period. At the same time appear bullae, or clay containers to hold the tokens. These, it is suggested, accompanied a delivery or shipment of goods, the tokens sealed inside the bulla providing a record of the transaction.

The connexion between these clay tokens and early Sumerian writing is that a number of the signs used in Sumerian script appear to be impressed or inscribed marks corresponding to the characteristic shapes of the three-dimensional tokens. Some thirty Sumerian signs at least appear to have a clay-token equivalent. It is suggested that the nexus between the use of tokens and the use of incised signs was the custom of impressing on the outside of a sealed clay bulla a record of the tokens it contained. This led eventually to the tokens themselves becoming redundant, and their replacement by the corresponding two-dimensional signs incised on clay tablets. Thus, according to Schmandt-Besserat, writing was born.

An original feature of Schmandt-Besserat's theory is that it dispenses with the need to appeal to the rebus in order to explain how signs which are apparently non-pictographic might have acquired their meanings. A paradoxical feature, however, is that although Schmandt-Besserat explicitly rejects the 'pictographic hypothesis', in fact the theory provides what is itself a pictographic explanation for the earliest written signs. For in effect these are two-dimensional pictograms representing the shapes of three-dimensional tokens. The difference is simply that the shape does not correspond directly to that of the animal or artifact which it signifies, but only to the shape of the arbitrary token. So the earliest written signs are themselves signs of signs: more precisely, pictograms of non-pictographic tokens.

The main weakness of the theory is that it leaves so many of the 1500-odd Sumerian signs unaccounted for; and for at least some of the unexplained signs pictographic origins seem *prima facie* to be undeniable. Furthermore, the evolution of the clay-token system itself bears witness to the incorporation of certain iconic signs at an early date. For example, already among the tokens dating from the ninth millennium B.C. are some which Schmandt-Besserat concedes to be 'schematic animal forms'. Later, when the products of the potter's workshop begin to figure prominently as artifacts, the clay tokens representative of various types of vessel tend to be, understandably, miniature three-dimensional versions of the vessel itself. It is hardly surprising that the corresponding Sumerian written characters turn out to look very much like outline drawings of those same vessels. In short, if we subtract the number of cases in which an independent iconic source might reasonably be postulated for the Sumerian written sign, the point Schmandt-Besserat is making begins to look less like an independent theory of the origin of writing, and more like a supplementary account of the progenitors of certain early Sumerian characters.

*

As regards the crucial transition from pre-writing to writing proper, all evolutionist historians of the subject find themselves in a quandary: they disagree about where to place it. For Cohen the rebus itself marks the advent of writing. But this is simply tantamount to a refusal to count as writing any systems which have no phonographic elements. For Gelb, writing proper is phonography, and the rebus principle does not quite achieve it, even though it marks a step along the way. Writing, in Gelb's view, emerges only with the earliest syllabaries. For Bloomfield, however, writing is achieved once a limited set of characters is fixed upon to represent words, whether or not the representation is in any way phonographic. But Bloomfield's seems to be very nearly a self-defeating criterion to invoke. For fixing upon a limited repertory of graphic symbols itself presupposes a prior period of experiment and fluctuation, and it is difficult to see why that prior stage cannot be granted the status of writing too. Indeed, unless the prior experiments were experiments *in writing*, it is hard to see the logic in this reasoning. That is to say, it is unclear how the fixing of an inventory of symbols could somehow make writing out of practices which had previously not been writing. Diringer hedges his bets on the question by distinguishing not only between 'embryonic' and 'true' writing, but also between 'true writing' and writing 'literally defined', the latter watershed matching Gelb's distinction between non-phonographic and phonographic representation. Schmandt-Besserat makes the advent of writing coincide with the substitution of two-dimensional impressions for three-dimensional tokens.

None of these evolutionary accounts can satisfactorily identify the transition from pre-writing to writing, because they do not squarely face the issue of what basic conceptual advance underlay the first attempts to produce written records. Consequently, they equate writing with logography, or else with phonography, or else with the introduction of phonographic elements into pictography, or else with the change from tokens to marks. But these are all quite arbitrary terminological decisions, and not solutions to the problem.

Instead of treating the problem as needing elucidation before any line of retrospective inquiry makes sense, they reverse the rationale of investigation and operate on the tacit assumption that if and when we know more about the facts of prehistory the nature of the problem will become clear, concomitantly with its correct answer.

Chapter Four

Writing as Representation

We have in use two different kinds of language, which have no sort of affinity between them, but what custom has established; and which are communicated thro' different organs: the one, thro' the eye, by means of written characters; the other, thro' the ear, by means of articulate sounds and tones. But these two kinds of language are so early in life associated, that it is difficult ever after to separate them; or not to suppose that there is some kind of natural connection between them.

Thomas Sheridan, 1762.

Writing, everyone agrees, did not originate with the alphabet. But it is our modern obsession with the superiority of alphabetic writing, together with our modern misconceptions of it, which are mainly responsible for the misleading way in which the problem of the origin of writing is usually approached. That it why it is of pivotal importance to understand both what alphabetic writing is, and also what it is not. For the traditional dogma that the letters of the alphabet 'represent' the sounds of speech leads automatically to casting non-phonographic writing retrospectively in a certain evolutionary role. It suggests, in effect, that if speech was not originally represented on the basis of identifying the sounds of the words uttered, then it must originally have been represented on some alternative basis. What alternative basis could this have been? There is, it is implied, only one plausible answer. That answer is summarised in the dictum which encapsulates the twentieth century's received evolutionist wisdom on the subject: 'At the basis of all writing stands the

Scribe taking a census of cattle. Thebes, *c.* 1400 B.C. British Museum.

picture.'[1] At best this statement captures only the technical aspect of the relationship between scriptorial and pictorial signs: at worst, it propagates a fundamental misconception. But it is plausible because it appears to be only what 'common sense' would lead us to expect.

When we see Egyptian hieroglyphs juxtaposed to Egyptian painting of the same period, as in a tomb dating from the middle of the second millennium B.C., there seems to a modern eye to be no question as to which is the more basic form of expression, which came first. It seems so obvious as not to require historical proof. We can readily imagine the hieroglyphs as the end product of some long process of simplification of the shapes already present in the painting. But we find it extraordinarily difficult to imagine the reverse. This

[1] Gelb, op.cit., p.27.

lively depiction of a cattle census in the Egypt of the Pharaohs could hardly be some weird and complex development of the shapes occurring in the band of hieroglyphs. Which came from which does not seem in doubt for a moment. And the connexion strikes us all the more forcibly in that we observe in the hieroglyphs as in the painting exactly the same emphasis on linearity, the same bold outlines, the same two-dimensional view of the world always seen sideways-on. Finding juxtapositions of this kind seems in itself eloquent evidence in favour of the view that writing derives from pictorial representation.

If further proof were needed, the subsequent history of writing appears immediately to supply it. The Rosetta Stone, for example, which gives the same text in three versions – hieroglyphic, demotic and Greek – apparently supplies all the comparison needed to demonstrate that as writing evolves the original iconic elements drop out and give place to arbitrary graphic notations of various kinds. So we seem to see a clear chronological progression from the pictorial to the non-pictorial in the evolution of script. It requires little imagination to supply at the top of the Rosetta Stone another and yet earlier band of carving pre-dating the hieroglyphs, and to suppose that this pre-hieroglyphic form of writing would have supplied even more direct visual clues to the subject-matter of the text.

A similar progression seems to be confirmed by early scripts from other parts of the world. In Assyrian, for example, it can hardly be a coincidence that the cuneiform character meaning 'heaven' took the form of a star; or that in China the character meaning 'moon' took the familiar crescent shape we see in modern Christmas cards and nursery-rhyme illustrations. In the course of time, evidently, the original iconic devices often became simplified out of all recognition: but there can hardly be any serious doubt that many of the characters used in early writing were originally iconic. It is often quite easy, even without special study, to see how the simplification of an original pictogram would have given rise to the configuration

The Rosetta stone, 196 B.C. British Museum.

of strokes which represent it in a later script. Unfortunately, the very ease with which this can be seen or imagined tends to encourage a hasty jumping to conclusions. It might even seem perverse to suggest that the thesis that 'at the basis of all writing stands the picture' captures only a half-truth; and that the other half of the truth is that 'at the basis of the picture stands writing'.

The thesis that writing, or at least certain forms of writing, evolved out of pictorial representation goes back to the Greeks. Little attention, however, has been paid to the connexion beween this view and theories of mimesis and symbolism in Greek antiquity. That connexion is already evident, nevertheless, in what Diodorus Siculus (3.4.) tells us about the hieroglyphs:

> Now it is found that the forms of their letters take the shape of animals of every kind, and of the members of the human body, and of implements and especially carpenters' tools: for their writing does not express the intended concept by means of syllables joined one to another, but by means of the significance of the objects which have been copied and by its figurative meaning which has been impressed upon the memory by practice. For instance, they draw the picture of a hawk, a crocodile, a snake, and of the members of the human body – an eye, a hand, a face, and the like. Now the hawk signifies to them everything which happens swiftly, since this animal is practically the swiftest of winged creatures. And the concept portrayed is then transferred, by the appropriate metaphorical transfer, to all swift things and to everything to which swiftness is appropriate, very much as if they had been named. And the crocodile is a symbol of all that is evil, and the eye is the warder of justice and the guardian of the entire body. And as for the members of the body, the right hand with fingers extended signifies a procuring of livelihood, and the left with the fingers closed, a keeping and guarding of property. The same way of reasoning applies also to the remaining characters, which represent parts of the body and implements and all other things; for by paying close attention to the significance which is inherent in each object and by training their minds through drill and exercise over a long period, they read from habit everything which has been written.[2]

[2] Tr. C.H. Oldfather, Loeb Classical Library, London, 1935.

Two features of this account are particularly worthy of note. First, it is evident that Diodorus thought that hieroglyphic writing simply bypassed speech altogether and attempted a direct representation of ideas. In this sense he had anticipated the modern concept of an ideogram. Second, the pictorial aspect of the hieroglyphs is, according to him, already of secondary importance. For the meaning of the characters cannot simply be 'read off' from their visible shape. We have to know, for example, that the crocodile is a symbol of evil, the eye a symbol of justice, and so on. These are not pictorial conventions as such, but independent metaphors based on association of ideas. So although the hieroglyphs are pictorially *recognisable*, they are not pictorially *interpretable*. Thus we encounter again in Diodorus the familiar Aristotelian doctrine of double symbolism or dual representation. This is the underlying theory which informs the recognition of hieroglyphs as a variety of writing in the first place, and hence sees them as comparable to the Greek alphabet. In both systems, ideas are represented only indirectly: in the one case through a representation of the corresponding spoken word, and in the other case through a representation of the corresponding visual image.

Recognising this theory behind Diodorus' description of the hieroglyphs brings us to acknowledge an explanatory relationship which is not immediately obvious: namely, that the 'pictorial' account of scriptogenesis is originally no more than an adaptation of a prior account of the relationship between phonography and speech. The tyranny of the alphabet here emerges in a subtler form than any so far considered. For how a pictogram functions as the expression of an idea is implicitly explained as being analogous to how a phonogram functions as the expression of an idea. In other words, writing is in effect being defined as the exploitation, in any appropriate graphic form, of the mechanism of double symbolism. But the doctrine of double symbolism was itself in the first place part of an account expressly designed to explain how the Greek alphabet worked.

This doctrine cannot, in turn, be divorced from Greek philosophical views about language and how language fitted in to the scheme of relationships involving human perception, memory and reality. Here the central notion in Plato is that of likeness or imitation, and in *Cratylus* we find an extensive discussion of the idea that a name is a special kind of imitation. It is not surprising, therefore, to find comparisons between language and painting figuring prominently in the debate between Socrates and Hermogenes about the 'correctness' of names. Is Hermogenes rightly called *Hermogenes*? The question initially sounds puzzling. For how can a man's name be correct or otherwise (granted that it *is* his name and we are not dealing with a case of mistaken identity)? Just how culture-bound the conundrum is can be judged by reflecting on the fact that it probably would not have puzzled Chief Buffalo Child Long Lance of the Blackfoot Indians for a moment. For Long Lance, who had doubtless never read Plato on the subject, explains in his autobiography how the purpose of a man's name is to 'tell the world what he is'.[3]

In the tradition in which Long Lance grew up, every Indian received at least three names during his lifetime. The earliest name a child was given was descriptive of some circumstance surrounding his birth. For example, a child born on a night when the midwife heard a wolf howling across the river was named 'Howling-in-the-Middle-of-the-Night'. His next name he would receive from his playmates during childhood, and likely as not it would not be flattering ('Bow Legs', 'Crazy Dog', 'Crooked Nose'). His third name depended on the showing he made in his first fight as a warrior against the enemy, and this name would be given to him by the chief of his tribe. If he fought well, he would receive a good name ('Uses-Both-Arms', 'Charging Buffalo', 'Six Killer', 'Good Striker'). But if not, he would be given a derogatory name. It

---

[3] *Long Lance*, p.20.

was taken for granted, however, that throughout his life a man should be given many opportunities 'to improve his name'. Subsequent deeds of valour would be rewarded by the bestowal of a 'better' name. None the less, any earlier names still remained his, so that a man's name constituted a record of his life and of his community's estimate of him.

Although the Blackfoot tradition of personal names was not the one Socrates was familiar with, it is interesting to note that the debate in *Cratylus* focuses upon a belief very similar to that which underlies the tribal practice described by Chief Buffalo Child Long Lance: that is, the belief that ideally a name should 'tell the truth' about its bearer. In *Cratylus*, this is extended from proper names to names of all kinds, and two ways in which names may 'tell the truth' are distinguished. One is essentially the Blackfoot way: a name may 'tell the truth' by being descriptive of what it designates. (*Bluebell*, on this view, is correctly descriptive of the flower it designates; whereas *redbell* would have been an 'incorrect' name.) But Socrates also discusses another way in which names may 'tell the truth'. A name may, by its consonants and vowels, represent the nature of what it designates.

There is a long discussion in *Cratylus* of the intrinsic properties of various consonants and vowels, and of their consequent fitness to represent certain ideas. The vowel *o*, for example, is held to be naturally fitted to express roundness, and therefore correctly used in names designating round things. Similarly, the lateral *l*, being pronounced with a gliding movement of the tongue, is naturally suited to employment in words designating gliding and similar movements. The assumption is that sounds will intrinsically 'represent' whatever their speech articulation most closely imitates. In short, we are dealing with a mimetic theory of natural representation.

In a memorable passage, Socrates expressly compares representation by words to representation by art:

Just as painters, when they wish to produce an imitation, sometimes use only red, sometimes some other colour, and sometimes mix many colours, as when they are making a picture of a man or something of that sort, employing each colour, I suppose, as they think the particular picture demands it. In just this way we, too, shall apply letters to things, using one letter for one thing, when that seems to be required, or many letters together, forming syllables, as they are called, and in turn combining syllables, and by their combination forming names and verbs.[4]

He goes on to argue that representation presupposes natural likeness:

Could a painting ... ever be made like any real thing, if there were no pigments out of which the painting is composed, which were by their nature like the objects which the painter's art imitates? Is not that impossible? ... In the same way, names can never be like anything unless those elements of which the names are composed exist in the first place and possess some kind of likeness to the things which the names imitate.[5]

By the end of the dialogue, nevertheless, we find Socrates forced to admit that appealing to a principle of natural representation does not after all take us very far in explaining language. Had he been acquainted either with the primitve rock paintings of South Africa or with the sophistications of a Picasso, he might perhaps have added that such a principle does not take us very far in explaining art either. But it is no coincidence that in Socrates' Greece language and art could both be conceived of as essentially mimetic; and no coincidence either that there for the first time in Western civilisation a primary oral culture was being definitively superseded by a culture based on the written word.

There is an essential connexion, as Irish Murdoch has

---

[4] *Cratylus* 424E. Tr. H. N. Fowler, Loeb Classical Library, London, 1926.
[5] ibid. 434A-B.

pointed out,[6] between Plato's objections to art and his mistrust of writing. In Book X of the *Republic*, Socrates invites us to compare painting with the making of furniture. The making of a bed is presented as a human attempt to imitate the eternal Form of a bed, the 'absolute, essential Bed', itself the work of God. A painting of a bed, on the other hand, is presented as merely a copy of the appearance of the man-made piece of furniture. Thus it is doubly removed from reality; for reality is to be found ultimately only in the Platonic domain of Forms. Furthermore, the painting of the bed is only an imperfect likeness of the bed-maker's manufactured article; for it will show the bed as seen from one angle only, omitting everything which is hidden from that particular viewpoint. Necessarily, therefore, the painting cannot represent the totality even of the man-made bed, but no more than a small part of it. It is a representation of a representation, and only a partial one at that. In short, it is a deception.

Similarly, writing is doubly degenerate as a representation of reality. The spoken word is misleading enough, for a name can capture only one aspect of the thing it designates. (The word *blackbird*, for example, alludes to the colour of the feathers; but the bird also has many other properties, of which the name tells us nothing.) The written word in turn is simply a copy of the spoken word. Socrates and Phaedrus agree that the written word 'may justly be called the image' of 'the living and breathing word'.[7] Here the parallel with painting might be pursued further than Plato takes it. Just as the painting of the bed represents the bed as seen from one angle only, so in alphabetic script the written word represents only one aspect of the spoken word; namely, how it sounds. That, Plato could well have argued in anticipation of Saussure, is to represent no more than its 'acoustic image': and perhaps even that only imperfectly.

[6] *The Fire and the Sun*, Oxford, 1977, p.21f., p.31.
[7] *Phaedrus* 276.

Writing, therefore, is a mimetic deception of the same order as painting. But this is not all. There is a further objection to both, which is put in its plainest terms in the *Phaedrus*. There Socrates compares writing and painting as 'lifeless' products. He points out to Phaedrus how the figures in a painting look like human beings, and yet remain silent whenever you ask them a question. It is just the same, he argues, in the case of writing. Written words appear to manifest intelligence, but if you ask them a question you get no answer. They remain silent like painted figures.[8] Again, the parallel could be pursued further than Plato chooses to pursue it. If life involves movement, then painting, as a static art form, is intrinsically incapable of representing it. Likewise, a sequence of alphabetic letters is a static form of representation, incapable of capturing the flow of articulation which is the essence of the spoken word.

Although the Stoics later took up the study of Greek phonetics and, as Diogenes Laertius (7.55) informs us, treatises on the subject were written by Diogenes of Babylon and Archedemus, the Greeks never made a great deal of progress in analysing the physiology of speech. The mechanics of pronunciation and the correspondences between articulatory movements and auditory effects remained largely unexplored. The basic reason for this failure has been recognised by modern scholarship. It was due, precisely, to the fact that 'the descriptive framework for Greek phonetics was the Greek alphabet'.[9] Consequently, the Greeks were led to ignore phonetic differences which were not reflected in Greek orthography. Although they were aware that Greek was pronounced differently in different parts of Greece, they paid attention to such differences only when this meant that the same word had more than one spelling. In effect, they accepted alphabetic spelling as giving a correct 'picture' of pronunci-

[8] ibid., 275.
[9] R.H. Robins, *A Short History of Linguistics*, 2nd ed., London, 1979, p.23.

ation, even to the extent of projecting on to the spoken word a hypothetical structure of discrete sounds matching the structural sequence of discrete letters in the corresponding orthographic forms. This fallacy, as Robins points out,[10] was never challenged in antiquity, and one finds it still accepted by Priscian, who likens the relationship of individual speech sounds in a word or sentence to the relationship of individual atoms in a physical object.

The fallacy is one which Plato could have made great play with, had he been aware of it. For it confirms his worst fears about the deceptions which may ensue from mistaking representation for reality, and underscores his parallel between writing and painting in a vivid way. One can imagine Socrates offering some sharp comments on the folly of attempting to train soldiers simply by showing them pictures of battles or to base medicine on a study of portraits of sick people. A similar analogy was to occur much later to Saussure, who remarked *à propos* of the importance attached to spelling: 'It is rather as if people believed that in order to find out what a person looks like it is better to study his photograph than his face.'[11]

*

Since in Plato's scheme of things even such arts as making beds or making swords are arts of imitation, there would be no place for making scripts at all unless that too were essentially mimetic. But it cannot have been just the influence of Plato which accounts for the persistence of this notion throughout the history of European culture. Its psychological roots are firmly planted in the elementary pedagogic practices involved in learning to read and to spell.

As children, we are taught that *c-a-t* is pronounced [kat] 'because' *c* stands for [k], *a* for [a], and *t* for [t], and 'because'

[10] loc.cit.
[11] F. de Saussure, op.cit., p.25.

the sequence [k] plus [a] plus [t] 'makes' [kat]. Whoever taught young Socrates to read doubtless told him a Greek version of the same story. But what does the child make of this curious rationale? The only analogue in a rather limited experience of interpreting marks on surfaces is likely to be that of drawing. The other drawn marks children encounter on surfaces are soon classified into three main groups: scribbles, pretty patterns, and pictures. Scribbles and pretty patterns do not 'stand for' anything; but pictures do. That is precisely what makes them pictures. Since letters too 'stand for' something, the obvious way of fitting them in to the child's world of marks is to construe them as drawings of things audible, as distinct from pictures (which are drawings of things visible). Thus 'recognising' the letters *cat* as a representation of the spoken word [kat] is exactly parallel to 'recognising' this other configuration of marks as a picture of a cat. For in both cases the child learns to demonstrate recognition of the representation by uttering the word [kat]. This is what adults will accept as proof that the child 'understands' the marks in either case.

Learning to spell leads to the same conclusion. Whether the equipment the child is given to use is a wax tablet and stylus, or pencil and paper, or chalk and blackboard, the criterion of being able to spell is invariably the ability to inscribe the right sequences of letters when the teacher produces the spoken samples. You are counted as being able to spell *cat* if you can write down that particular sequence of letters whenever the word the teacher pronounces is heard as [kat]. That is the archetypal 'spelling test'.

Again, the number of ways open to a child to make sense of what is going on in this form of exercise is extremely limited, and an obvious way of construing it is to suppose that one is being asked to draw a picture of some kind. But of what? If the test word is *cat*, the drawing required is obviously not a picture of the animal. That would be to confuse the spelling lesson with the art lesson. So it must be a drawing of what the teacher pronounces in saying *cat*. What else could it be?

This interpretation is apparently confirmed by various strands of supporting evidence. For example, it will count as a 'mistake' if you fail to round the *c*, with the result that it looks too much like an *r*. This is wrong, because *rat* is a different word from the one you were asked to spell. But what exactly is the difference? Clearly, it is the difference between the beginning of [kat] and the beginning of [rat], two words which are otherwise 'the same'. So *c* must be the drawing of one of these two distinct things, whilst *r* is the drawing of the other. This hypothesis is in turn confirmed by a recurrence of the same difference between spelling *can* and *ran*, and similar rhyming pairs.

So there seems to be in the child's experience a ready-made answer to the question 'What are the letters drawings of?' This answer, moreover, is confirmed rather than abandoned when the child encounters spellings which run counter to the basic pattern of a one-one correspondence between pronunciation and letter. For these acquire the status of 'exceptions' to an otherwise regular system. They are what makes spelling 'difficult', and also what makes reading 'difficult'. The letters that turn out not to correspond to the facts of pronunciation at all are thus aptly called 'silent' letters.

If we are taught to put 'silent' letters in spelling certain words, why are we not taught to put in 'silent' strokes when drawing the corresponding objects? The question is a good one, although it must rarely if ever occur to children to ask it. That is perhaps just as well, because most of their teachers would be hard put to it to give an answer. The knot in your shoelace is spelt with a silent *k*; but can we imagine a system of drawing which demanded in the corresponding picture a visually superfluous loop or squiggle? ('You haven't drawn the shoelaces very well, darling. You forgot to put in the extra bit on the knot – you remember, the bit that isn't there?') Hardly a plausible scenario, even for modern science fiction.

The implausibility and the implications of that implausibility, once fully grasped, must lead us eventually to realise not that the parallel between spelling a word and drawing a picture only goes so far, but rather that there was no parallel to begin with. The trouble does not lie in the bizarre quirks of English orthography. For it would make no difference if English spelling were as regular, consistent and economical as you please: except that, if it were, then the invalidity of the 'parallel' would be that much harder to spot. But it is hard enough to spot in any case, because it turns out to be educationally advantageous to ignore it. The pedagogic process is helped, not hindered, by assuming that the parallel holds.

Speaking, comprehension of speech, reading and writing are four extremely complex activities. If society demands that children master them, anything which facilitates the task of both teachers and learners will stand a good chance of meeting with approval. The pedagogic process is thus predisposed to favour ideally simple correspondences between the spoken and the written word: they are easier to handle for both parties concerned. The notion that each letter stands for one spoken segment involves an ideally simple correspondence of this kind. Pupils are taught to look for, at least to hope for, such correspondences, and this inculcates the feeling that getting to grips with the written word is basically a matter of 'recognising' such correspondences. Success in the 'recognition' task in turn inculcates the feeling that what is being grasped is some basic representational relationship of the kind which allows us to recognise correspondences between other configurations of marks and the things they are intended to represent. However mistaken that impression may be, if it is psychologically conducive to confidence in tackling the problems of learning to read and write, eventual success in reading and writing can only reinforce it.

Recent work on dyslexia supports the probability that what underlies the lay conviction that not all words are 'spelled as they are pronounced' or 'pronounced as they are spelled' is that reading involves, for most people, mastering a set of correspondences between speech-sounds and written characters. This is what would in part explain the relationship between the types of disability known as 'surface dyslexia', 'phonological dyslexia' and 'deep dyslexia'. In surface dyslexia, patients have a problem with reading words which have an 'irregular' spelling. In phonological dyslexia, the relevant difficulty is one of reading words of which the spelling is 'regular', but which are unfamiliar. In deep dyslexia, patients are typically unable to read orthographically regular nonsense words, or to match such words to familiar ones having the same pronunciation (*chare*: *chair*). These complementary types of disability suggest that some patients have lost and others retained their grasp of some set of 'grapheme to phoneme' conversions as part of their normally available equipment for reading. The 'grapheme-to-phoneme' conversions are neuro-anatomically locatable, according to recent models, in the angular gyrus of the cerebral cortex.[12]

Evidence from Japanese dyslexics further suggests that phonographic and logographic symbols are separately processed by readers acquainted with systems which use both, as in Japanese *kana* and *kanji* writing.[13] Deficiencies in one are not automatically paralleled by deficiencies in the other. Thus, evidently, there are quite specific neurolinguistic dimensions to the problem of the origin of writing, as well as to the progression from logographic to phonographic systems of writing. But most important of all is the conclusion that without the invention of writing and its cultural institutionalisation, there would be no such medically recognised disability as 'dyslexia'. Aristotle knew nothing about dyslexia,

---

[12] G.W. Hynd and C.R. Hynd, 'Dyslexia: neuroanatomical/neurolinguistic perspectives', *Reading Research Quarterly*, Vol. 19 No.4, 1984, pp.482-98.
[13] S. Sasanuma, 'Acquired dyslexia in Japanese: clinical features and underlying mechanisms'. In M. Coltheart, K. Patterson and J.C. Marshall (eds.) *Deep Dyslexia*, London, 1980, pp.48-90.

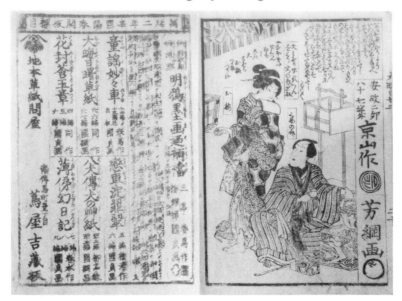

Japanese *kana* and *kanji* characters in a mid-nineteenth-century text.

despite its Greek name. But what light does this modern research throw upon the Aristotelian doctrine that writing represents speech? It suggests that Aristotle misconstrued correlational patterns between letters and sounds as evidence of an intrinsic representational relationship.

Even if we are not immediately persuaded that the notion of letters representing parts of spoken words is just a pedagogically inculcated illusion, it must at least be seen to be doubtful whether the claim that a certain letter represents a certain phonetic unit requires appeal to no other concept of 'representation' than is involved in claiming that a certain drawing represents a cat, or that a certain line in the drawing represents the cat's tail. If the drawing 'copies' in various particulars the shape of the cat, what is it that the letter or sequence of letters copies?

Recognising the possible need for a different concept of 'representation', or perhaps a different concept of 'mimesis', does not by implication criticise anyone for failure to distinguish in the first place between the way a drawing represents something seen and the way writing (allegedly) represents something spoken. For not even the most committed advocate of the view that letters represent phonetic units supposes that both letters and phonetic units are alike audible; whereas both the cat and the drawing of the cat are at least both visible, and there is consequently a common visual basis for assessing to what extent there is a likeness between them. With phonetic units and letters, the case is somewhat different, and no one denies it. That is not what is at issue. So 'What do letters copy?' is not to be interpreted as a rhetorical question. On the contrary, it must be taken seriously before we have any right to reject it and pass on to consider non-mimetic modes of representation.

The question of 'phonetic iconicity', as it is sometimes called, can be interpreted in two ways, depending on whether the iconicity in question is articulatory or acoustic. It is possible, as David Abercrombie points out,[14] to devise systems of phonetic notation based on indicating the positions of the organs of speech, or systems based on indicating properties of the resultant sound waves. The latter possibility is illustrated by Potter, Kopp and Green's system of notation based on letters derived from the shapes of simplified sound spectrograms.[15] This, however, presupposes the availability of sophisticated equipment for acoustic analysis, and any suggestion that what underlies the letterforms of the alphabet might be some kind of intuitive apprehension of 'acoustic shapes' verges on fantasy. Articulatory iconicity seems much the more promising candidate, and has attracted a considerable amount of attention. Almost all claims for an

[14] In a paper contributed to the seminar on 'Letterforms as articulatory diagrams', London, 1977.
[15] R.K. Potter, G.A. Kopp and H.C. Green, *Visible Speech*, New York, 1947.

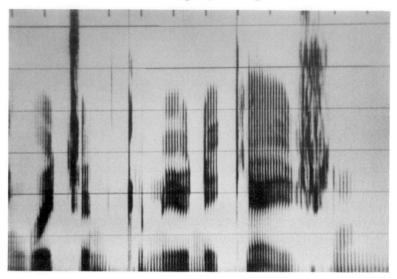

Visible speech: a second spectrogram with 500 Hz analysing filter. Phonetics Laboratory, Oxford University.

iconic origin of letters of the alphabet start from the premiss that the audible sound has a visible or at least visualisable correlate, namely the position or movement of the speech organs; and it is this which the shape of the letter 'copies'.

In *Cratylus* where no consistent distinction is drawn between phonetic units and letters, there is only a hint of how Socrates might have dealt with the question. But it would be consistent with the notion that articulatory movements are naturally expressive of basic concepts or properties (as the tongue movement of Greek *rho* for expressing motion)[16] to suppose that, similarly, certain letter shapes are naturally appropriate to express the corresponding articulatory movements. An ideal alphabetic letter, from this point of view, would be *o*; for the shape of the character copies the visible rounding of the lips, which in turn, as Socrates suggests, is a movement naturally

[16] *Cratylus* 426C.

expressive of roundness.

The notion that the 'ideal' or 'primitive' alphabet would have originally consisted of simple drawings of the appropriate lip and tongue positions for the different speech sounds is among those used by Kipling in his fictional account of the efforts of Taffimai and her father. It had been for centuries an idea recurrent in speculations about the origin of the alphabet. For example, in 1772 Charles Davy advanced the theory that the Greeks had retained only seven of the letters in the alphabet originally introduced by Cadmus: gamma, delta, eta, kappa, lambda, rho and tau. These original seven were then supplemented by another fifteen, constituting 'a new kind of picture-writing (ἐν γράμμασι μίμησις, in the strictest sense), that served to point out sounds instead of things'.[17] Thus the vowel [a], according to Davy, 'was pronounced with a considerable aperture of the mouth ... and the air directed against the palate'. This the Greeks represented by the letter alpha, and it seemed obvious to Davy that 'nothing could more exactly represent the opening of the lips in profile for the purpose, than the character of this letter reclined'. He hypothesised that this was the earliest way of writing the alpha, which 'was afterwards erected for the sake of taking up less room'. The cross bar he explained as indicating 'the situation of the teeth'. Thus the history of alpha could be sketched diagrammatically in the manner shown in Figure 5.

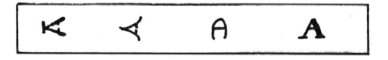

Fig. 5 (after Davy 1772)

[17] *Conjectural Observations on the Origin and Progress of Alphabetic Writing,* London, 1772, p.83ff.

Similarly, Davy held that the vowel represented by epsilon was 'pronounced by a moderate aperture of the lips, the tongue being placed straight out, so as to give the air, forced from the trachaea, a direct passage, neither throwing it upwards or downwards; and this position of the tongue, nearly at an equal distance from the roof and bottom of the mouth, was pointed out by the middle stroke in the center (sic) of the curved line, or between the parallel lines in the square letter'.

Fig. 6 (after Davy 1772)

Davy proceeds in similar fashion to explain the shapes of iota, omicron, omega, upsilon, beta, mu, pi, phi, zeta, nu, xi, sigma and theta. Some of the letters cause him more trouble than others, and he is at rather a loss to explain how the three labials, beta, mu and pi, all originally diagrams of lip closure, have become differentiated. On questions of tongue position his notions are in some instances curious; but no more curious, it might be urged, than those the Greeks might have had. All in all, he makes out a case which cannot be dismissed out of hand.

Davy's idea was by no means original. A similar claim had been made for Hebrew characters in the seventeenth century by Jean Baptiste van Helmont. The interest shown in phonetic iconicity as an explanation of the alphabet at this period was doubtless connected with attempts to develop 'rational' systems of notation on phonetic principles, such as that outlined by John Wilkins in 1668 in his famous *Essay Towards a Real Character*, and the introduction of various early systems of phonetically-based shorthand, including those of Tiffin (1750), Lyle (1762) and Holdsworth and Aldridge (1766). These were the precursors of more well-known nineteenth-century shorthands, such as Pitman's and Bell's.

The kind of system Pitman devised is sometimes called 'analogically iconic',[18] but the term is misleading. What Pitman did was to give certain shorthand shapes a constant articulatory value. Thus, for example, a straight line always indicates a stop consonant, a curved line indicates a fricative, and so on. But this simply means that a given symbol consistently provides certain physiological information about the articulation it designates. It does not make the symbol itself iconic in any sense, unless a further mimetic explanation is provided of the iconicity of adopting a straight line for stops, and a curve for fricatives.

The theory of phonetic iconicity has been taken up again in the twentieth century in a somewhat modified form, and extended to such diverse scripts as Arabic, Sumerian and Japanese. The claim nowadays made is usually a weaker one than formerly: it is to the effect that there is a significant tendency in the writing systems of the world to adopt as symbols those characters which can be interpreted as articulatory diagrams relevant to the pronunciation in question. This, although an interesting claim in its own right, does not provide any direct support for the thesis that the alphabet was originally devised as a phonetically iconic system.

What emerges fairly clearly from a survey of claims about the (possible) phonetic iconicity of the alphabet is that they are all based, in one way or another, on reducing pronunciation to what can be seen or felt concerning the positions or movements of the articulatory organs. The reduction always proceeds in that direction. No one suggests that a mark on a surface has a natural phonetic correlate unless there is an underlying reduction in the other direction to support it. In this regard the most intuitively convincing case for phonetic iconicity – the

[18] See D. Abercrombie, *Elements of General Phonetics*, Edinburgh, 1967, pp.117-18.

letter *o* – is also the most eloquent. If the human vocal apparatus were so designed that a back vowel of this type were normally articulated without visible lip-rounding, no one would be claiming that the letter *o* is phonetically iconic at all. Even the notion of acoustic iconicity depends on the reduction of properties of sound waves to a visual representation by the mechanism of the spectrograph. 'At the basis of all writing stands the picture' is a dictum which lends itself to interpretation in more ways than one.

Granted all this, it is still legitimate to ask what underlies the lay conviction that some languages or at least some words are 'written as they are spoken', or 'spoken as they are written', whereas others are not. The answer can hardly be in doubt. It is a question of recognising discrepancies or inconsistencies in the systematic correspondence between pronunciations and the use of letters. Any word of which the spelling cannot be predicted on the basis of its pronunciation or vice versa may be felt to be in some degree 'irregular'. Awareness of such 'irregularities', however, may itself be conditioned by habits of spelling, or so it is often claimed. 'Every German who has not enjoyed a training in the physiology of sound,' asserted Paul, 'is convinced that he writes as he speaks.'[19] He will fail, for example, to realise that the final consonant in *tag* is a different sound from the medial consonant in *tages* because he is accustomed to spelling both with the same letter. Similarly, many educated English speakers probably fail to realise that there is any phonetic difference between the final sibilant in *cats* and the final sibilant in *dogs*, in spite of their orthographic identity. In these particular examples, however, orthography is not the only factor which might contribute to a failure to recognise phonetic distinctions. The conviction that the final consonant of *tag* and the medial consonant of *tages* are 'the same sound' may in part be based (i) on the fact that this type

---

[19] H. Paul, *Principles of the History of Language*, tr. H.A. Strong, London, 1890, p.38.

of phonetic variation involving consonants in final and medial position is quite a regular pattern in spoken German, and (ii) on the recognition of *tag* and *tages* as forms of 'the same word'. In the case of *cats* and *dogs*, the final sibilant is not only identically spelt but is recognised as the 'same ending' in both cases, namely the plural suffix. In contemporary psycholinguistics, connexions of this order are often translated into the fashionable jargon of 'mental representation'. It will nowadays be claimed that what a previous generation of linguists used to call allophones and allomorphs are merely surface variations of units which have a single mental representation for the speaker at some cognitive level or other. On this view, doubtless, it might even make sense to claim that what writing 'really' represents are the speaker's mental representations themselves. But *homo scribens* is already given to enough mysticism about writing, without the further encouragement of psycholinguistic fantasising of this order.

Discrepancies between spelling and pronunciation, however, bring into focus the whole question of the extent to which practical orthography does function in accordance with the Aristotelian doctrine that alphabetic writing represents speech. Any final judgment upon this question will depend on how broadly or narrowly we are prepared to interpret the term 'speech'. When speech is contrasted with writing, it is usual to concentrate upon the most obvious differences between the corresponding forms of physiological activity. Speech is thought of in terms of movements of the vocal tract, and writing in terms of movements of the hand holding a pen or other instrument. But this dichotomy oversimplifies. We speak and write with our whole body, in just the same way as a stroke at tennis or at billiards is played with the whole body, and not just the limb controlling the racquet or cue. Speech is in this sense no less visible than writing. When we talk face-to-face to another person, movements of the head, eyes, facial musculature, hands and arms, as well as general posture, count for no less than the activity going on in the vocal tract. From this point of view, the theory of phonetic iconicity is roughly on a par with claiming that when the scorer enters a dot in a bowler's analysis in the cricket scorebook, what he is doing is drawing a picture of the look of blank surprise on the bowler's face that no run was scored from that particular delivery.

The question how far writing represents speech, however, is most frequently construed as a rather narrow question about accuracy of orthography as an indication of pronunciation. There are different ways in which even this narrow question may be interpreted, depending on whether what is under consideration is phonetic accuracy or phonemic accuracy. Not even the most enthusiastic champion of the alphabet would claim that it is a system designed to represent speech with complete fidelity to phonetic detail. Even allowing for the limitations inherent in any static symbolisation when it comes to portraying dynamic processes, and for the limitations inherent in the capacity of any set of discrete elements to capture the non-discreteness of continuities, the alphabet as such is not equipped to render any of the very many important features of pronunciation which fall under the heads of stress and intonation. In this connexion it is interesting to ask oneself what conclusions a Martian might draw if alphabetic writing were the sole source of evidence available to Martians about the languages of Earth, and if it were believed on Mars that the alphabet must be a system able to cope with all the phonetic vagaries of Earthly speech.

Among the first conclusions the Martian would draw, presumably, are that stress and intonation play no role in speech. Earthlings would be envisaged as endowed with organs of phonation which were limited to producing an even, monotonous vibration, with abrupt qualitative transitions between one segment and the next. (One imagines this might pose some problems for Martian physiologists in determining the hypothetical configuration of the human vocal tract.) Martian philologists would be led to conclude erroneously that, for example, the English noun *entrance* and the English verb *entrance* were phonetically identical. More generally, they would be unable to detect patterns of allophonic variation of the type which distinguish, say, the initial consonant of English *leaf* from the final consonant of English *feel*. They would be quite unaware that there are sounds in French which never occur in English, and vice versa. They would seriously underestimate the number of English phonemes, and would be oblivious to the fact that different varieties of spoken English utilise different phonemic contrasts. They would suppose that *pair, pear* and *pare* were all pronounced differently, and that *cough* rhymed with *rough*. In short their attempts to reconstruct phonological systems for the languages of Earth would go far astray, and they would have scarcely any information about what speech sounded like at all.

A defender of the Aristotelian doctrine might perhaps object that it misses the point to cite the many instances and respects in which, for historical and other reasons, traditional spelling is badly adapted to representing the pronunciation of a language as currently spoken. For these cases are violations or misapplications of the alphabetic principle: but what is at issue is a question about the alphabetic principle itself.

To this objection, a reply might be given along the following lines. Bell called his shorthand system *Visible Speech*.[20] It is both alphabetic and iconic in its letter shapes, which copy configurations of the glottis, palate, tongue and lips. Furthermore, it would doubtless be possible to adapt Bell's system by the use of varying letter-faces, and greater flexibility of disposition of the characters on the printed page than simple linearity allows, in such a way as to incorporate all the main distinctions of stress and intonation that are significant in, say, spoken English. But to cite an ideal notation of this kind as a vindication of Aristotle would be both an anachronism

---

[20] Alexander Melville Bell, *Visible Speech: the Science of Universal Alphabetics*, London, 1867.

and an irrelevance. No one doubts that, within the inherent limitations imposed by alphabetic notation, it is possible to devise a system which will 'make speech visible' in the sense claimed by Bell's title. It will give, in other words, a visible iconic analysis of the articulatory postures involved in speaking. That is not the question, however. The question is whether alphabetic writing, in its original or any of its traditional forms, was in fact designed to function as a system of 'visible speech'. Certainly it was and is used to *record* speech; but that is a different matter. For speech, as noted earlier, cannot simply be equated with pronunciation; nor is preserving a record to be equated with giving an articulatory analysis. Moreover, whether recording speech was in any case the earliest or primary function of writing seems open to doubt.

The doctrine that writing represents speech fudges the issue of exactly what represents what. Is it the form of the letter *p* which represents the outline of the closed lips when we say *pin* (as earlier theorists of phonetic iconicity held)? If it is not the form of the letter which represents anything, what else does? Similarly, if it is not the shape of the closed lips which is represented, what else could it be? Is it the movement of the lips towards closure, or the closure itself, or the labial release from the closed position? Or is it neither the articulatory movement nor the articulatory posture but the characteristic disturbance of air which accompanies it? And if so, precisely what features of this vibratory disturbance are represented? (We must note in this connexion that it will be circular to reply: 'Just those features involved in the pronunciation of the letter *p*.' For what is at issue is precisely how to construe the concept of pronouncing a letter.) Or is what is represented neither an articulatory nor an acoustic event, but just the auditory impression of these events which the ear registers? If so, how do we characterise this impression? Does it include the audible aspiration which accompanies the bilabial stop in *pin*? Or is that accompaniment left orthographically unrepresented? Again, could it be that what is represented is none of the foregoing, but a familiar sensation derived from the muscular contractions and other motor efforts which are habitually brought into play in the articulation of a bilabial voiceless stop? Finally, does the *p* represent some combination of all these various things; and if so, which combination?

The list of queries is not intended as an indirect *reductio ad absurdum.* On the contrary, it is perfectly possible to propose quite specific answers; the point is that such answers, or alternatives, *must* be proposed if the claim that writing represents speech is to be taken seriously. It is clear, for example, that Davy in the eighteenth century was making a claim about the relationship between letterforms and articulatory postures. It is equally clear that for Socrates in the *Cratylus* the elements of the spoken word were certain articulatory movements. Such proposals may be criticised or faulted on various grounds: but unless answers along these lines are forthcoming to questions about what represents what, the issue of the phonetic accuracy or otherwise of written representations cannot even get off the ground. Furthermore, any defence of the thesis that these are cases of mimetic representation will depend rather crucially upon the particular answer given. Davy's position, for instance, makes it quite clear in what respect we are to look for likenesses. But if he had proposed that the letter *p* iconically represents a combination of acoustic and auditory features, it would then be entirely unclear what we are supposed to be looking for as evidence of likenesses.

It may be tempting, for those determined at all costs to salvage something from the Aristotelian doctrine, to take refuge behind the semiological altar and plead that Aristotle and his contemporaries patently failed to distinguish between speech (in the Saussurean sense of *parole*) and the language (in the Saussurean sense of *langue*). So what they were 'really' trying to say, in their unenlightened pre-revelation way, was that spelling reflects elements of *langue* (as distinct from the pronunciation of those elements). In other words, there may at this point come a temptation to abandon the mimetic theory altogether and retreat to the safer ground of saying that writing does not after all 'represent' speech in anything like the sense in which the drawing represents the cat, but that a representational relationship nevertheless holds at a much more abstract level. It might be urged that we should construe the alphabetic principle as being, or as being analogous to, the phonemic principle. That is to say, a correlation holds (ideally a one-one correlation) between the members of a certain set of written characters and the members of certain sets of contrastive units operative in pronunciation. Thus the letter *p* will 'represent' on this view an abstraction defined, as it were, by the aggregate of cases in which the pronunciation of *pin* is counted as minimally distinct from that of other forms (*bin, tin, sin, fin, gin,* etc.).

Construing the alphabetic principle in this way, however, opens a Pandora's box of problems. One is the problem of deciding whether this manoeuvre still leaves us with anything we can reasonably call a 'representational' relationship at all. Rather, what we seem to be doing is defining one particular purpose for which it would, if we wish, be possible to use alphabetic letters. But that requires, for its justification, something analogous to the modern theory of the phoneme; and it is far from clear, to say the least, that the inventors of the alphabet were inspired by anything like modern phoneme theory. A no less serious problem is that even if they were thus inspired, they must have been plagued by exactly the same set of unresolved difficulties which modern phoneme theory has brought out into the open. These difficulties highlight the fact that, whatever criteria are adopted to determine contrasts in pronunciation, it is always in principle possible to produce alternative phonological analyses of any extensive sample of phonetic data.[21] This erodes the concept of a 'representational'

[21] Y.R. Chao: 'The non-uniqueness of phonemic solutions of phonetic systems', *Bulletin of the Institute of History and Philology*, Academia Sinica, 1934, Vol.IV, Part 4.

relationship even further. For it is simply playing with words to claim that the letter *p* 'represents' the conjunction of whatever possible alternative phonological analyses of the corresponding phonetics are available.

Counterevidence of an even more damning kind for the hypothesis that writing represents *langue* rather than *parole* comes from written languages which recognise grammatical distinctions unknown in the related oral vernacular. A well-known example is that of French tenses. The written language includes sets of forms (called the 'Preterite': e.g. for the verb 'to have', *j'eus, tu eus, il eut, elle eut, nous eûmes, vous eûtes, ils eurent, elles eurent*) which simply do not occur in modern spoken French at all, other than in reading aloud written texts. It is not the case that such forms are 'unpronounceable' in the sense that they lack any agreed phonetic counterparts. On the contrary, that they have such phonetic counterparts, in spite of the fact that these are forms which do not occur in everyday spoken French, shows that what we are dealing with is a set of conventions for rendering pronunciations on the basis of written characters. (It is irrelevant that the spelling of these forms happens to include a high percentage of 'silent' letters.) As long as people fail to draw the distinction between *langue* and *parole*, or some equivalent distinction, the move of treating writing as a representation of *langue* rather than *parole* is not open to them. But the moment they draw that distinction and wish to use it to explain features of the relationship between speech and writing, they find themselves hoist with the petard that what are culturally recognised as spoken and written forms of 'the same language' constitute semiologically different systems.

A parallel from non-alphabetic writing may be apposite here. Many elements of writing can indeed be matched up with features of a particular (spoken) *langue*, rather than features of its associated *parole*. But there are others which match neither. For example, the determinative signs employed in Egyptian hieroglyphic writing include one which identifies a word as the name of a goddess, queen or princess, as in Figure 7.

Fig. 7 (after Andrews 1981)[22]

Here the last two symbols have no phonetic or phonemic or morphological value whatsoever. It is a convention of writing, not of *langue*, by which they are here appended to the name *Cleopatra*. But how do we know, it may be asked, that Egyptian priests when reading out such an inscription would not have put in some honorific title (such as 'Lady' or 'Dame') to correspond to the presence of the determinatives in the script? The answer is that we cannot know this for certain: but even if they did, or some of them did, that would still not justify construing determinatives as graphic abbreviations for titles. To see why not, it may be instructive to consider a hypothetical parallel. Suppose it were the normal practice to write the letter 'T' in English on the end of every name of a town or city: *LondonT is the capital of England*. Now it might be the case that in reading such a sentence aloud, people often read it as 'London-tee is the capital of England', or even 'London-town is the capital of England'. But that would not make the appended letter 'T' into a sign 'standing for' some elided or omitted syllable in the normal 'T-less' sentences of the spoken *langue*. For *ex hypothesi* the addition of the 'T' in writing is obligatory, even when taking down spoken sentences which lack any such syllable.

Could we not, alternatively, construe the 'T', like the hieroglyphic determinative, as standing for some grammatical category, such as 'proper name'? Even Saussure, after all,

[22] C. Andrews, *The Rosetta Stone*, London, 1981, p.17.

admitted abstract entities in grammar as part of *la langue*.[23] To justify this, it would as a matter of course be necessary to demonstrate that the names in question, whether proper names, names of goddesses or town names, did in fact have a distinctive grammar in the language in question, independently of their written form. But suppose this could be demonstrated. What would then be wrong with treating the graphic symbol in question as standing for a particular category in *la langue*? Nothing; except that this new move does not vindicate the Aristotelian doctrine in the least. For that is not how the doctrine claims that the alphabet works. Writing is supposed to represent *words*, not abstract classifications of words, which would be something altogether different – a metalinguistic enterprise even further removed from what is audible or visible.

Nor would appeal to the *langue/parole* distinction get over difficulties of a more obvious order, such as the fact that the distinction between capital letters and small letters corresponds to no spoken distinction at all. The point here is not simply that we pronounce particular words (such as *bible*) in exactly the same way, regardless of whether they are written with a small or a capital letter; but rather that there is no parallel in speech to the 'small vs. capital' distinction itself. Appeal to the *langue/parole* distinction does not account either for the fact that contrasts between different scriptorial forms may be used to express messages in ways to which there is no oral counterpart. For instance, a recent property development was advertised in newspapers by a picture showing a doorplate bearing the legend:

GRAB THIS
VNIQUE BVSINESS
OPPORTVNITY

[23] F. de Saussure, op.cit., Part II, Ch.VIII.

The prestige value of the pseudo-Roman lettering, combined with the social meaning of the doorplate, and the deliberately grating hard-sell jargon of the inscription, combine to make this another text which defies reading.

*

Rather than drive any hypothetical defenders of the Aristotelian doctrine further into intellectual corners of this kind, it is more worth while to ask where the doctrine itself goes astray. The answer is that it goes astray by misconstruing a complex of pedagogically inculcated practices as evidence of a representational relationship between writing and speech, while at the same time reserving the right not to come clean on the twin questions of what represents what, and how. We are expected, in short, to have an 'intuitive' grasp of this representational relationship, and not to question it. No visiting Martian anthropologists could hope for a clearer indication that what they are investigating is not a rational theory of any kind, but a prestigious piece of cultural mythology.

Even if we grant all this, it still does not tell us 'the truth' about the alphabet. What is the truth? Certainly it is part of the truth that the alphabet is not a mimetic representation of anything; and claims to the contrary must in the end distort mimesis itself into a conceptually unrecognisable shape. But what else? A first glimpse of what else is involved we can get by reflecting on the fact that, as far as is known from available historical evidence, the earliest form of the alphabet had no vowels.[24] This may sound like an unexpected appeal to 'historical facts' in the midst of a historically sceptical inquiry. So it may be prudent to add that it will make no difference if Diringer's generation of scholars are subsequently proved wrong and still earlier forms of the alphabet are discovered

---

[24] D. Diringer, *The Alphabet*, London, 1948, pp.217-18.

which do have vowels. For if that happens, we shall still be left
with a choice between two possibilities. Either the early
vowel-less alphabet developed independently; or else it
somehow simply 'dropped the vowels' of its parent form.
Whichever is the case, the essence of the present argument
would be left unaffected. The argument, to state its conclusion
in advance, aims to show that if there is any sense to be made
of the thesis that writing represents speech, it is not the kind of
sense which will afford the Aristotelian any comfort at all.

The explanation usually offered for a primitive vowel-less
alphabet is that originally 'the alphabet was created for
Semitic languages'.[25] It is not suggested that the Semitic
languages originally had no vowels, nor even that the vowels
played no role in the grammatical structure of the Semitic
languages. But it is held that Semitic vowels are not in some
respects indispensable, and this claim is often backed up by
reference to later orthographic practice in Hebrew and Arabic,
where vowels are omitted because, as Diringer puts it, 'the
Semitic languages are based chiefly on roots, which give us the
fundamental conception, and are represented by consonants,
while the vowel sounds give us only the complements, the
details, such as the part of speech, the voice, the mood, the
tense'. We are told, in short, that all this 'grammatical'
information can normally be inferred from context in the
Semitic languages – perhaps not invariably, but at least
generally enough to cause the native reader of these languages
no severe problems of interpretation for most of the time as far
as written texts are concerned. The implications of this
'explanation' are many and fascinating. In effect, we are again
being invited to subscribe to the theory that 'at the beginning
of writing stands the picture'; but this time in a more subtle
disguise. For what Diringer calls the 'fundamental conception'
(invariably represented by the consonantal root in Semitic) is
in the great majority of cases a conception which abstracts

[25] ibid., p.217.

from such issues as whether we are dealing with a thing or an action, an agent or a patient, actuality or possibility, the past, the present or the future. Now what could be the model for such an abstraction? Only the picture. For it is paradigmatic in the case of the picture that it makes no sense to ask whether this scene is *represented as* a hunter shooting a deer, or a deer being shot by a hunter; or whether *what is represented* is the shooting or the shot; or whether the picture *represents* it as past, present or future. These are all intrinsically unanswerable questions: which is to say that they are nonsense questions, at the same time as admitting that we may have all kinds of attendant clues and general principles (both pictorial and non-pictorial) which would enable us in any particular instance to propose reasonable answers to them.

Smith may say quite confidently, for example, that this picture represents a past event, because he recognises it, for all kinds of reasons, as a picture of the signing of Magna Carta. But that is quite different from saying that he recognises the technique as one which is pictorially characteristic of the Middle Ages. And it is different again from denying that it is an earlier prophetic picture of the signing of Magna Carta on the ground of not believing that painters in the eleventh century or earlier had historical foresight. So, curiously, the timelessness of a picture links up thematically with the a-grammaticality of Semitic consonantal roots and their spelling. Moreover, it links up in more ways than one. For the question is whether a 'consonants only' system is capable of 'spelling' anything at all unless we are operating by definition with a system in which things other than consonants just do not count as spellable.

It is also often suggested that a 'consonants only' system would not have worked orthographically for a language like Greek, which does not have a comparable system of consonantal roots; and this would explain why, when the alphabet was borrowed by the Greeks, it was found necessary to introduce characters for vowels. What goes for Greek allegedly goes equally for other Indo-European languages: thus English would be hard put to it to use a 'consonants only' system to distinguish between *bitter, better, batter* and *butter*. But if this is true at all, it is only a half-truth. To borrow Bolinger's example,[26] we have no insuperable difficulty in reading, without prior warning or training in the 'shorthand', *Y mst b crfl wth sch ppl.* On the contrary, modern systems of 'speed writing' capitalise on the fact that we can do without vowels and, in many cases, consonants; but still be left with a form of alphabetic writing which is perfectly comprehensible. This still does not answer the question 'What does it spell?'

It would be grotesque to suggest that all this flexibility is possible only because the supposed 'omissions' are interpretable by tacit reference to a 'full' representation in which the omitted elements are present. Sacrosanct teachings about 'ellipsis' in the European grammatical tradition are doubtless responsible for a psychological shoring-up of such assumptions. Fortunately, everyday experience – if we are wise enough to pay attention to it – teaches us that we do not respond to the cry 'Help!' by puzzling over whether it 'stands for' a sentence which might be represented more fully as 'I want help', or 'You want help', or 'What an extraordinary thing help is'. The reason why the very suggestion is absurd is that at no point in our education were we taught – nor did we try to work out for ourselves – the rules of reduction which would be necessary to operate such imperfect systems of communication. Nor were we ever privileged to be presented with that architecturally complete 'full system' which must stand logically as the base on which permissible reductions are to be made. The same general principle applies to alphabetic writing. No one can reduce our salary from £10,000 to £7,000 if we were only getting £4,000 in the first place.

Now the glimpse of truth which such considerations afford us is this: that there are many phenomena of speech which

---

[26] D. Bolinger, *Aspects of Language*, 2nd ed., New York, 1975, p.488.

alphabetic writing can be taken to indicate, but without letters to represent them in any shape or form at all, mimetic or otherwise. It suffices that we 'read in' the relevant information, which is not explicitly laid out for inspection, or may even be deliberately withheld. Of this, the use of the asterisk in order to avoid offending Victorian sensibility is a paradigm example. The rationale of this use of the asterisk perhaps reveals more about the psychology of *homo alphabeticus* than any other single orthographic convention known. Rather than introduce a substitute asterisk into forms like *f*cking*, it ought presumably to have been more discreet simply to proceed orthographically straight from *f* to *c* with no gap. What the asterisk does is actually draw attention to the omitted vowel, and thus invite the reader to 'supply' it. This does not, incidentally, put the asterisk semiologically on an equal footing with the letters of the alphabet: for it is a mere sign of omission. What invites further reflexion, however, is the fact that when the 'Victorian' use of the asterisk is kept to a minimum, it is always in English a variable for a vowel. It is difficult to resist the attraction of the speculative question as to what connexion links this evidence that vowels are 'rude' letters and consonants 'decent' to the omission of vowels from the original alphabet. Perhaps it is simply that in order to pronounce vowels you have to open your mouth, whereas to pronounce most consonants you have to close it. Opening and closure have always been symbolically fraught movements. Whatever the answer, it is clear that we live in an orthographic world of consonantal chauvinism. (Who will start a movement for 'vowels' rights'?)

A further glimpse of the truth is afforded by pondering the fact that the alphabet as such contains no symbols for word-division, either internal or external. The hyphen is a modern accretion which has never been systematically integrated into the repertory of letters. The same is true of the apostrophe, currently undergoing a crisis in English writing, which hinges on whether it ought to be extended from marking genitives to marking plurals. (*Budgerigar's for sale* announces the notice in the pet shop window; but it will be no use going in to inquire whether it is the budgerigar's seed or its cage which is on offer.) Even more striking is the late standardisation of the practice of leaving spaces between words. One is tempted to compare the introduction of the space as a word boundary to the invention of zero in mathematics; but the parallel is superficial. The space is not one additional alphabetic character, but the absence of any character. Its introduction points up a lacuna in writing which is eloquent in more ways than one.

Putting the absence of division-symbols together with the original absence of vowels at least points us towards various things the inventors of the alphabet were clearly *not* interested in 'representing'. They were not interested in representing what would nowadays be called morphology, or the internal grammatical composition of word forms, or systematic variation between related word forms. Nor were they interested in representing the syntagmatic composition of word groups. Nor, as noted earlier, were they interested in representing features of stress and intonation. But most paradoxical of all is the conclusion that they were not interested in the alphabetic principle itself. Or at least, not the alphabetic principle as that is usually interpreted by modern scholarship: that is, the principle 'one letter: one sound'.

The alphabetic principle, according to Diringer, was never realised with complete success in any form of the alphabet; but it was nevertheless a goal towards which much progress was made. In the perfect alphabet 'each sound must be represented by a single constant symbol'.[27] It is ironic that this idea continues to survive at the present day, when the reasons why such a goal is impossible to achieve had already been stated with great lucidity in the nineteenth century by Hermann Paul. Once those reasons are appreciated, it becomes rather

[27] Diringer, op.cit., p.218.

implausible, to say the least, to continue to interpret the origin and development of the alphabet in terms of attempts to achieve that goal. Inventors do, indeed, sometimes set themselves impossible targets: but it is gratuitous to attribute that error retrospectively to the inventors of the alphabet by saddling them with an 'alphabetic principle' which there are no reasons at all for believing they would have endorsed. What Paul pointed out was: 'A word is not a united compound of a definite number of independent sounds, of which each can be expressed by an alphabetical sign; but it is essentially a continuous series of infinitely numerous sounds, and alphabetical symbols do no more than bring out certain characteristic points of this series in an imperfect way.'[28] It would have been better still if Paul had qualified this statement, for as it stands it appears to accept commitment to the idea that it is indeed the sound of a spoken word which spelling is an attempt to capture. A more judicious formulation might perhaps be: 'Even if we wished to use sequences of alphabetic letters as notations to "stand for" stretches of continuous sound varying qualitatively over time, the most we could hope to achieve would be to arrange our symbols in sequences corresponding to the perceived order of selected 'points' or transitions in the phonetic continuum.' In other words, there is no question of using a separate symbol for each sound, because sounds are not discrete segmental units. Or if they are, there must be an infinite number of them in even the 'shortest' spoken word: for the same reason that there is an infinite number of sequential divisions in an inch. The so-called 'alphabetic principle' consequently enshrines a fundamental misconception about the nature of sound. It perpetuates the old 'atomic' fallacy which received its definitive formulation in the fifth century at the hands of Priscian. 'Just as atoms come together and produce every corporeal thing, so likewise do speech sounds compose speech as it were some

[28] Paul, op.cit., p.39.

bodily entity.'[29]

What, then, were the originators of the alphabet interested in? The best answer we can hope to have comes from considering what might be called the 'internal' semiology of the alphabet itself. Two features immediately claim attention. The first is that the letters of the alphabet are not hierarchically or relationally ordered. True, there is a traditional 'alphabetical order': but that is something externally imposed on the system. It derives neither from the structure of the system nor from its function. 'A, B, C, D, E, F ... ' is not like '1,2,3,4,5,6 ... ', nor like 'January, February, March, April, May, June ... '. The letters of the alphabet are independent and equipollent characters. Second, they are meant to be used in combination with one another for purposes of writing. It is only an accident that a single letter ever suffices to spell a word. If the letters had not been meant to be used in free sequential combination, it would have been necessary to invent many more of them, as Sequoyah soon discovered in devising his system for Cherokee. The second principle may sometimes be obscured by the fact that in no written language we know are anything like the full number of distinct letter-sequences actually used. Furthermore, we sometimes find quite fixed sequential restrictions, of which the fact that *q* must always be followed by *u* in writing English words would be one example. But it is important to see that these apparent contradictions of the principle of free sequential combination are not inherent in the alphabet itself: they derive from particular linguistic uses to which the alphabet is put.

The entire architecture of the alphabetic system rests on the application of these two principles of equipollence and free sequential combination. The question can now be put: what communicational purposes is it likely that such a system would have been designed to serve? In order to propose a convincing answer, it becomes necessary to resolve a preliminary but

[29] Robins, op.cit., p.23. (Priscian, *Institutiones Grammaticae* 1.2.4.)

crucial issue. This issue is simply whether we are assuming that the inventors of the alphabet simultaneously invented writing, or whether we are assuming that the inventors of the alphabet were already acquainted with prior forms of writing of a non-alphabetic kind. If we make the former assumption, that puts an end to any possibility of elucidating the matter further. For it stretches credulity beyond any reasonable limits to imagine pre-literate people sitting down and devising *ex nihilo* a writing system with the semiological structure of the alphabet. Even the Sequoyahs of this world (and so far there has only been one) do not do anything comparable. Sequoyah's case has been rightly described as one of 'stimulus diffusion': which means that he had started by borrowing the idea of the cultural practice of writing from somewhere else, and set himself the task of devising a system which would make it applicable in his particular case. The origin of the alphabet, it seems reasonable to assume, was also a case of stimulus diffusion. Its originality lay, precisely, in devising a new system for writing which eliminated some of the disadvantages of existing systems. But it is quite implausible to equate that originality with the adoption of the misguided ideal 'one letter: one sound' for reasons in addition to those already mentioned.

If we think of the problem as one of devising a writing system more economical than, but equivalent to, pre-alphabetic writing systems, it becomes clear that the most natural step would not be a Gargantuan leap to a spelling principle like 'one letter: one sound'. For we know of only two kinds of writing with which the inventors of the alphabet were likely to have been acquainted: syllabaries and hieroglyphics. The question therefore arises: what kind of linguistic equivalence do these kinds of writing have when compared with each other and with alphabetic writing? The answer cannot be in much doubt. All three are equivalent at a linguistic level of great practical utility, but for which we have no current linguistic term: and this is, significantly, because modern linguistics insists on talking about language in terms of hierarchies of discrete units. The nearest approach to what we want would be to call it the level of 'word identification'; but this is obviously unsatisfactory in view of the long debates which have racked modern linguistics about the definition of the 'word'. There would be no point in plunging again into these endless controversies here.

Perhaps the terminological difficulty can safely be ignored provided it is made clear in non-technical language what this equivalence amounts to. We are looking, in effect, for a level of correspondence between pictograms, syllabic characters and alphabetic spelling. For the sake of focussing on a concrete example, let us suppose we are comparing (i) a pictogram which comprises a circle with rays radiating from it, (ii) a syllabic character which looks like an ampersand, and (iii) the alphabetic letter-sequence *sun*. Now the only reason we would probably be comparing these three in the first place would be in the context of some practical enterprise of the kind nowadays generally called 'translation'. That involves, essentially, the reformulation of linguistic messages for the benefit of those unacquainted with the linguistic system in which the messages were originally delivered. As it happens, there is every reason to believe that the alphabet was devised in a polyglot cultural situation which made translation a necessity of paramount practical importance; but although that is a fact of great historical significance, it is not essential to the present argument. The considerations invoked here would still in principle apply even if the systems in question were being used to write one and the same language (however 'one and the same language' is defined). What is essential to the comparison is simply that we have some practical reason for raising the question of linguistic comparability between our three graphic signs.

The nub of the comparison is this. In all kinds of ways there will be non-equivalences between the three signs. For they belong to quite different systems of writing. Automatically, therefore, one pictogram will contrast with another in ways which cannot be paralleled in the dimension of contrasts between one spelling and another. But now we are setting aside these differences and looking for what might be called 'equivalences notwithstanding the differences'. We can establish one such equivalence – not necessarily the only one, but perhaps the most psychologically salient one – if we can establish that it serves the purposes of communication to treat the three signs as ways of designating 'the same thing'. Let us call that same thing 'the sun'. What the equivalence involves might in practice be manifest in all kinds of ways, ranging from statements about the local weather to statements about the entire planetary system or about people's religious beliefs. But what it does not involve, necessarily, is an assumption that any of the written signs for 'the sun' has one and only one phonetic correlate. The great mistake about the alphabet is the persistent belief that it constitutes *eo ipso* a phonetic notation, as distinct from pictograms or ideograms, which constitute non-phonetic notations. This is simply a fourth-form howler of the most elementary order. That it can be perpetrated at all by academically distinguished scholars is symptomatic of the accumulated pressure of cultural bias which distorts modern intellectual efforts to come to terms with language.

There is no basis for assuming that the pictogram as such is open to many different phonetic interpretations whereas the alphabetic sequence *sun* is not. This remains true even when we specify that these graphic signs are to be interpreted as written designations of 'the sun' (whatever that means). For we all know, when we come to think about it, that in different linguistic communities and subcommunities different pronunciations may co-exist under the umbrella of one and the same spelling. So why should we think there is any basic difference *in this respect* between pictographic writing, syllabaries and the alphabet? The answer is that the collective wisdom of those who educate us teaches us this doctrine. Why? That is another question: and one we cannot indefinitely evade. But, for the moment, it suffices to put the point in the following way. The alphabet was not devised by people committed to setting up a science of phonetics *avant la lettre*. They were interested in 'writing as writing', not in 'what it sounded like'. And writing 'as writing' had been for many centuries previously independent of the spoken word. That independence gave it, indeed, its basic linguistic advantage over speech. Hence it is particularly perverse of modern scholarship to present progress in human written communication as consisting in working towards devising one system, namely the alphabet, which was an improvement over its predecessors in being specifically tied to pronunciation. 'Standing history on its head' is a metaphor which does scant justice to cultural acrobatics of this order: but it is difficult to think of a better one.

None of this amounts to a denial that alphabetic writing has anything to do with speech, any more than it amounts to a denial that pictographic writing has anything to do with sight (although the latter claim is often, misguidedly, made in order to distinguish the two). The truth is that both forms of writing have to do with speech, although both are in principle independent of speech. What needs further thought is *what* exactly they have to do with speech and *how* exactly they are independent of it. Treating the inventors of the alphabet as precursors of the committee which designed the International Phonetic Alphabet (IPA) is what stands history on its head. The IPA is undeniably a form of the alphabet; but the alphabet is not undeniably a form (imperfect, rudimentary, or otherwise) of the IPA.

Alphabetisation is essentially a problem of re-deploying existing symbols in such a way as to reduce their number, but at the same time lose few or none of the facilities of 'word identification' which the previous writing system afforded. In essence it does not differ from the reduction of logographic systems to syllabaries. That is why the so-called 'alphabetic principle' is a misnomer. How the reduction may best be carried out will depend on the language and the previous system concerned. One possible reductive method is that of acrophony, which is in effect the notational counterpart of 'Able, Baker, Charlie ... ' spelling; but it is not the only one. If the earlier writing is already syllabic, it may be possible to re-deploy the characters in such a way that some combination of any two from a subset of the original inventory will replace all the single characters previously used, but without loss of word identification. It would be perfectly possible to do this, for example, with Sequoyah's Cherokee syllabary; but it was a step Sequoyah never took. Such a reduction could be effected in a variety of ways. If the result is to be internally 'regular', however, and avoid too many 'arbitrary' combinations, the new system must in effect re-align the correspondences between the pronunciations of words and their written form. This may sound like the introduction of a phonemic principle; but it is not. A spelling which is 'phonemic' (by modern standards) might well be the result; but 'non-phonemic' solutions are equally possible. This depends, again, on the language. A much cruder way of reducing a syllabary to an alphabet would simply be to ignore the phonetic distinctions associated with differences between certain syllabic symbols; for example, ignore the vocalic differences. Something like this may well have happened to produce the early vowel-less North Semitic alphabet. There is thus a sense in which alphabetisation, far from implementing an ideal notation to render pronunciation, may in certain cases be an 'anti-phonemic' and even 'anti-phonetic' process.[30]

The mistake made in assuming the alphabet to be an *intrinsically* phonetic notation is a complex one, to which all kinds of historical circumstances contributed. But it is

---

[30] It may even be an 'un-natural' one if phoneticians are right in believing that syllable-sized segments, rather than single consonants or vowels, are more plausible minimum units for the processes involved in speech production and speech perception. This would fit in with the fact that syllabaries have been developed independently in various parts of the world, whereas alphabetic writing appears to have been invented just once.

conceptually analogous to believing the reference grid on a street map to represent features of the townscape on a par with the lines showing existing streets. Certainly the grid has something to do with the streets. What is utterly mistaken is to believe that the lines of the grid 'represent' streets themselves. Somewhere in between is the muddle generated by the fact that once you have accepted the grid, then you can not only describe the disposition of streets by reference to the lines on the grid but also, having done that, describe the grid itself by reference to the way it 'intersects' the streets. The muddle can, from one point of view, be described as just a failure to distinguish between the marks which constitute the grid and the marks which map the streets – both of which appear as black lines on the same white surface. But to think it is no more than that is already to subscribe to a semiology of maps which is so simplistic as merely to shift the constructional problem from one intellectual quicksand to another. In the alphabetic parallel, it is a case of alphabetic symbols projecting 'imaginary' grid divisions on to the phonetic townscape. The important point to grasp is that although two modes of description thereby become available in either case, one mode is parasitic upon the other. Anyone who does not understand that has not understood anything worth understanding about the relationship between streets and grid. It might, for instance, be possible to get so muddled as to think that the streets themselves were a map of the grid. Oddly, this is the kind of mistake which modern linguistic theorists are fond of attributing to those who, in their view, misconstrue the relationship between speech and alphabetic writing. What they fail to see is that this is simply their own mistake reversed in the alphabetic looking-glass.

Chapter Five

The Great Invention

Writing is universally allowed to be the noblest Invention that
can possibly be conceived.

W.F. Mavor, *c*. 1785.

'It *is* a great invention,' said the chief of little Taffimai's tribe:
but the reluctance of modern historians of writing to face the
fact of its being an invention is remarkable. Writing can
hardly have 'evolved' on its own out of primitive drawing, any
more than the internal combustion engine evolved out of the
kettle. Cohen accepts the term *invention*, but equates that
invention with the rebus, which is merely the adaptation of an
already existing sign. Others put the word *invention* in scare
quotes, as if its use in connexion with the origin of writing
were figurative. At the other end of the spectrum, Gelb denies
outright that writing was invented;[1] and this on the curious
ground that all so-called inventions are simply improvements
on what preceded them. Thus presumably, in Gelb's view, the
human race has never actually invented anything at all.

There is an important element of truth in the contention
that writing was invented when a certain systematic
correlation was established between graphic marks and words.
But it merely devalues this truth to anticipate history and
make a teleological ideal of the alphabet, which is in effect
what happens when the capacity of the system for indicating
pronunciation is erected into the criterion for recognising
writing as such. For it builds into the definition of writing *ab*

[1] Gelb, op.cit., p.199.

initio our modern notion of correspondence between writing and pronunciation, which is itself alphabetically based and alphabetically biassed. We do not know, and never shall know, what concept of 'pronunciation', if any, was entertained at that remote period by the human beings who invented writing. So a less question-begging point of departure is necessary for our inquiry.

If we suppose that writing developed out of pictures, as many claim, it is interesting to consider what stages of transition might in principle have linked the two. Could there be a form of symbolisation which was equally interpretable as pictorial or scriptorial: or such that the question as to which was which became in principle undecidable? We may, for convenience, visualise the problem by imagining the Rosetta Stone with an indefinite number of upper, more primitive bands above the hieroglyphs, of which the top band is undoubtedly a pictorial version of 'the same text'. The question would then be at what point in the intermediate bands do we recognise the transition from pictures to script?

It would simply postpone the problem to say that we would detect the transition by noting the gradual introduction of non-pictorial elements into the successive bands of engraving. For the question is how we can distinguish between the pictorial and the non-pictorial, granted that an originally pictorial configuration can survive in recognisably the same form long after it has ceased to function as anything other than the sign for a specific word. Furthermore, it is unclear how we would distinguish between a simplification of the pictorial elements and the introduction of scriptorial elements.

An interesting example of the progressive simplification of a pictorial sign is provided by the history of Delft tiles.[2] Here the original fleur-de-lis corner eventually became so modified over the centuries that it is no longer immediately recognisable as a fleur-de-lis and merges with, or evolves into, other types of

[2] D. Korf, *Tegels*, 2nd ed., Bussum, 1961.

corner design, notably the 'ox head'. Correspondingly, it is possible to imagine that in the Rosetta Stone example we might encounter a chronological progression from 'recognisable' to 'unrecognisable' pictures, but have no ground for equating this progression at any clearly demarcated point with the introduction of scriptorial signs. A degenerate pictorial form does not automatically become writing. If it did, the Delft fleur-de-lis corner ought to have become a word somewhere between 1650 and 1725.

The realisation that staring hard at this hypothetical Rosetta Stone will not solve our problem might prompt us to think that the answer must be to ask a hypothetical ancient Egyptian – or series of Egyptians, of the appropriate periods – to tell us at what point in this series of bands writing first appears. But this will not do either, for various reasons. First, we are not entitled to assume that the hypothetical Egyptians in question necessarily have a clear verbal distinction in their language corresponding to our modern differentation of pictures from writing. For all we know, they might have gone on using a single term indifferently for both, long after we ourselves had recognised, say, the emergence of hieroglyphs. Or they might have distinguished verbally in some other way which cuts across our own division between the pictorial and the scriptorial. So a pre-requisite of our posing the question would be to make sure that they understood what was being asked. The problem with this is that we are not quite sure ourselves what is being asked before clarifying to our own satisfaction exactly what we mean by the distinction in question. Until we have, whole dynasties of willing Egyptians will be of no help.

The problem of undecidability might be approached from another angle by considering the familiar case of illuminated capitals in medieval manuscripts. Suppose we have a capital showing the snake in the Garden of Eden suitably writhing in the form of the letter 'S'. Now this is clearly both a picture and also a letter. It makes no sense to ask *which* it is. However, it is

Fig. 8. Evolution of the fleur-de-lis corner (after Korf).

easy to imagine a transitional series of related capitals for which the question might arise, since there is no doubt that a capital could show what was clearly a snake, although not in the form of the letter 'S'; or, alternatively, a capital might be clearly a letter 'S', but no longer recognisable as a snake. The precise configurational points at which the illumination ceases to be clearly a letter 'S' will obviously be different from those at which the illumination ceases to be clearly a snake. *But could we imagine cases in which those sets of points coincided exactly?* Can we then go on to imagine that this was the case for all the characters in a given system of writing? If so, then we should presumably be dealing with a writing system formally indistinguishable from a system of pictorial representation; at least, on one level. This qualification needs to be added, because if the characters in question correspond to our letters of the alphabet, or something similar, then combinations of them which 'make sense' as writing will not necessarily 'make sense' as picture-sequences, and vice-versa. Having got thus far, however, let us venture one further large imaginative stride and consider whether we can stretch our fantasy to encompass a case where even this last difference is resolved. That is to say, the sequences make sense regardless of whether they are taken as pictures or as writing. And, finally, why not suppose that, whether taken as pictures or as writing, a sequence interpreted either way always 'means the same thing'? If we can imagine all this, then we can imagine a case of absolute isomorphism between pictorial and scriptorial communication. Let us call this state of affairs 'graphic isomorphism'.

Perhaps, however, our imagination got stranded somewhere along the road which led to this final isomorphism. Or perhaps it could take those last steps only with an uncomfortable feeling that somehow we had now lost the distinction between pictorial and scriptorial altogether. But have we? The question is of interest; for if it were possible to envisage our primitive ancestors starting with systems which were 'ambiguous' as between pictorial and scriptorial interpretations, then splitting off pictures from writing or writing from pictures would become a matter of the progressive introduction of elements which were not subject to isomorphic interpretation. But let us for the moment give the imagination a rest and try to see in a more humdrum way what the semiology of this proposal amounts to.

A writing system, whatever else it may be, is a system of signs; and all systems of signs presuppose communicational purposes for which they are used. This commonsense observation does not at first sight appear to take us very far towards identifying what is special about writing. But it may take us further than we suppose if we think through its implications on the basis of some very simple examples of communicational problems.

Let us suppose it is desired to make a permanent record of the moves played in a particularly important game of chess. The equipment available to do this consists of an ordinary snapshot camera and an unlimited supply of film. The problem, therefore, is how to make an indefinite number of still photographs function as signs indicating the course of play in the game.

A straightforward plan would be to start by taking a sequence of photographs showing the position of pieces on the board after each move. For that purpose, it is not essential that the photographs themselves should be taken in the same chronological order as moves in the game; nor that they should be photographs of the actual chess board and pieces used. All that is essential is that the photographs should eventually be 'read' as following one another in the same sequence as moves in the game. Otherwise, they will be simply an unordered set of images of a chess board, which can be shuffled at random. A photographer who took a still photograph of each successive position in the game 'on the spot' as it occurred would have all the material required to record the game; but in order for his photographs to constitute the desired record they would have to be marked or presented to the viewer as constituting one specific sequence. In this sense, photographs of the actual game in progress are only one subset of the potentially infinite set of photographs which could provide an accurate record of the game in question.

This essential condition for providing a record of the game (namely, that the sequence in which the photographs are 'read' matches the sequence of moves) may be referred to for convenience as the *matching condition*. Fulfilment of the matching condition, however, does not require that the photographs be photographs of the game itself in progress, nor even that they be photographs at all. The same condition can be fulfilled by drawings and diagrams of various kinds: for instance, diagrams of the kind commonly found in books on chess. These normally represent the chess board as an eight-by-eight two-dimensional array of squares, and the various chessmen as iconic two-dimensional shapes of the pieces in question.

Medieval iconic representation of a board game, probably chess. Fourteenth-century Flemish illuminated manuscript. Bodleian Library MS Bodley 264, fol. 112r.

It goes without saying that in order to fulfil the matching condition, each individual photograph or diagram must itself fulfil what may be called a condition of *perspicuity*. Clearly, it is possible to take any number of photographs of a chessboard which, although capturing the shapes which come within the range of the camera's lens, do not show unambiguously which chessman stands on which square, or show this for some but not all areas of the board. A photographer who photographed the chessboard from angles which made it impossible to determine the exact location of the chessmen would have failed to satisfy one perspicuity condition, and his photographs would consequently be inadequate to provide the desired record of the game. The same is true of any drawings or diagrams of the board.

It follows, then, that photographs as such – even photographs taken on the spot as play progresses – have no privileged status as signs of the series of moves which occurred in the game. On the contrary, in order to qualify as a record of the game, on-the-spot photographs must fulfil exactly the same conditions as non-photographic signs of various kinds. It is not the photograph which stands here as the ideal form of sign, but, on the contrary, the conditions for communicational significance which determine what a photograph is capable of showing. The conventional symbols by which chess manuals indicate the moves in a game are not substitutes for photographs of the board, much less 'degenerate' versions of what the camera sees. The boot is on the other foot. What the camera 'sees' will only provide a record of the game, provided that the photographs supply information equivalent to that of the conventional symbols of the chess manual.

One idea we can dismiss, therefore, is that iconic images enjoy some kind of natural priority as a form of sign. If there is any basic mistake underlying the picture-theory of the origin of writing, this is it. The supposed pictorial priority is quite illusory. Everything depends on what the signs are intended to communicate. The point is of crucial importance as regards the notion of a primitive 'isomorphism' between pictures and writing.

Now it would be just as absurd to devise a system of chess notation which failed to distinguish, say, between a pawn and a queen as it would be to take photographs which did not show which was which. This requirement for an adequate chess record (i.e. to distinguish pawns from queens) is clearly demanded by the structure of the game itself. This is not, however, the case for all features of an adequate chess notation. For example, the so-called 'algebraic' system assigns a letter of the alphabet to each file and a number to each rank, thus enabling any square on the board to be identified by means of a letter-numeral combination (*f3, b4,* etc.). But while it is important to be able to identify each square by some means or other, the method of adopting letters to designate files and numbers to designate ranks has no special significance in terms of the way chess is played. Giving every square its own name would serve the purpose just as well. Here the algebraic system itself, by designating the square in this particular way, superimposes a structure of its own upon the distinctions required for an adequate notation. There may be certain advantages to the algebraic system (for instance, visualising the exact location of a given square on the board may be easier with letter-numeral combinations than with other systems of designation) but these advantages are external to the demands imposed by the structure of the game as such.

This distinction between structurally necessary and structurally superimposed features applies to all systems of signs, although it may not always in practice be an easy distinction to draw. Armed with this distinction, nevertheless, we shall at least be able to go back to the question of isomorphism between the pictorial and scriptorial and make some progress with it.

One reason why we may initially find the notion of graphic isomorphism hard to get to grips with is that our modern

experience of the enormously diverse functions of pictorial and
scriptorial signs makes it difficult to imagine how they could
naturally coincide, or what kind of society it would be which
might develop such signs, or for what purpose. But the notion
of the natural coincidence – or rather inseparability – of
pictorial and scriptorial functions is less problematic if we think
of it in an appropriate context of culture. It is less problematic
still if we are willing to recognise at the outset that there are
just two primordially distinct varieties of autonomous visual
sign. These two varieties have no universally accepted
designations. Here we may call them 'emblem' and 'token'.
How emblems differ from tokens will become clear in what
follows. The emblem is an archetypal constant, and the token
an archetypal variable (although not in the sense in which
modern mathematical logic uses these terms).

Psychologically, graphic isomorphism might even be
regarded as the most natural form of symbolism for a culture
in which, for instance, names and totems are treated as
complementary aspects of identity. If a tribe has the wolf as its
totem, then the wolf mark, whatever form it takes (not
necessarily an iconic form), simultaneously 'stands for' the
totem animal and the name 'wolf' as complementary aspects of
the identity of the Wolf tribe. The question as to 'which' aspect
it stands for does not even arise in such a culture; indeed, it is
anachronistic to describe the relationship by using terms like
'standing for'. For the name is not treated as just a convenient
verbal label any more than the mark is treated as just a
convenient visual logo for purposes of classification. Both are
integral to the essential spirit or being of the people who
identify themselves thus. In a cultural context of this kind, the
totem mark is in one sense automatically a symbol of a
symbol: but not in the Aristotelian sense, which already
presupposes the distinction between the spoken and the written
word.

This form of symbolism is symptomatic of something which
goes far beyond the limits of totemism in the strict

anthropological sense: it reflects a more widespread attitude to the mystical status of names, images and identities in both pre-literate and literate cultures. It is, *par excellence*, the symbolism of the emblem. Emblematic symbolism may extend, with varying degrees of sophistication, to a whole pantheon of gods, spirits, forces of nature, significant events, and particular individuals (especially rulers) as well as particular places (especially sacred places). It is often bound up in various ways with word magic and practices of name-giving. It reflects, fundamentally, a mentality for which reality is still not clearly divisible into language and non-language, any more than it is divisible into the physical and the metaphysical, or into the moral and the practical.

Emblems of this culturally and psychologically primitive kind are the remote ancestors of many kinds of visual device which still survive in the modern world, ranging from national flags and family crests to trade marks and religious symbols. These latter-day descendants share at least one semiological feature with the primitive emblem: they are identificational constants. They have a fixed value inasmuch as they are intended to be identified with just one nation, family, religion, cause or commercial product. Unlike the primitive emblem, however, they are signs which have long since become integrated into the ways of sophisticated and literate civilisations. They are no longer graphically isomorphic signs. The name of the national flag, for instance, will typically not be identical with the name of the nation: the flag will have its own name ('Union Jack', 'Stars and Stripes', etc.). Moreover, the flag as a visual sign will belong to a form of communication now implicitly defined by contrast with writing. This is the inevitable fate of the emblem once writing becomes institutionalised as a cultural practice with its own norms, conventions and metalanguage.

In a pre-literate culture, however, emblems (whether of the sun, the moon, animals, plants, rivers, gods or mortals) provide a set of graphically isomorphic archetypes which form a natural basis for any potential development in the direction of literacy. Seen in this light, the problem of the origin of writing becomes in part that of determining how emblematic forms might develop non-emblematic uses. In other words, the seed of writing will lie in the possibility of opening up a gap between the pictorial and the scriptorial function of the emblematic sign. Its germination will be the process which then leads to development of a distinct set of graphic signs, which are used solely in association with the scriptorial function.

The obvious social path which such a development might follow would involve the gradually extended use of emblematic signs for purely 'utilitarian' purposes – purposes of which the utilitarian nature is not at first clearly distinguishable from its ritualistic or quasi-magical embedding. One such cultural breeding ground – and arguably the most ancient – lies in the various practices, beliefs and methods associated with counting. Almost certainly *homo sapiens* mastered the use of numbers before mastering the use of letters. What is being suggested here is something else: that the human race had to become numerate in order to become literate. No society which could not count beyond three ever achieved writing; at least, not by its own efforts.

Nor is it any coincidence that counting involves signs of the other primordial variety: the token. The prompter in a modern recording studio who silently holds up two fingers to indicate that there are just two minutes of 'time' left is using, whether he realises it or not amid all the technology provided by successive revolutions in human communication, the archetypal system of visual signs which was one of the precursors of writing. 'Gesture counting' of quite complicated varieties is still widely used in the marketplaces of Africa,[3] and of other countries where the conflict of spoken languages presents a communicational barrier to buying and selling.

Counting is in its very essence magical, if any human

[3] C. Zaslavsky, *Africa Counts*, Boston, 1973, p.46ff., p.238ff.

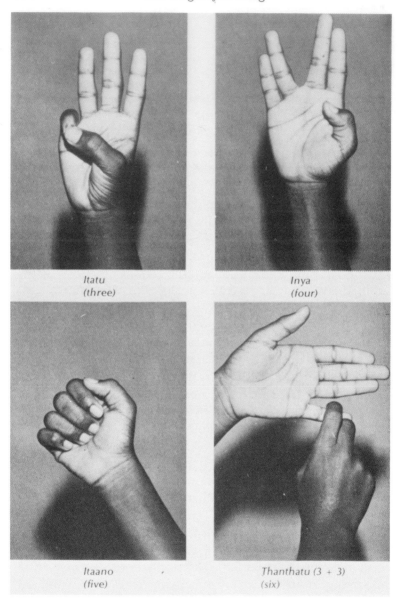

Itatu
(three)

Inya
(four)

Itaano
(five)

Thanthatu (3 + 3)
(six)

Kamba gesture counting. From C. Zaslavsky, *Africa Counts* (1973) p. 244.

practice at all is. For numbers are things no one has ever seen or heard or touched. Yet somehow they exist, and their existence can be confirmed in quite everyday terms by all kinds of humdrum procedures which allow mere mortals to agree beyond any shadow of doubt as to 'how many' eggs there are in a basket or 'how many' loaves of bread on the table. Furthermore, numbers are instantly and ubiquitously available for every conceivable counting operation, like spirits that can be conjured up at will. They transfer readily from dealing with eggs, to loaves of bread, to people in a community, to stars in the sky. No wonder that in many cultures they have the power to tell one's fate and forecast the future, as only supernatural beings can.

A society which keeps count of its flocks and herds in the manner Schmandt-Besserat describes as in use in prehistoric Mesopotamia may still entertain all kinds of superstitions about numbers; but at least it has got past the stage of believing that it is 'unlucky' to count living creatures, as some societies believe. To that extent it has already developed a 'utilitarian' attitude towards numbers. Likewise, it must have a 'utilitarian' attitude also towards the clay tokens used in the reckoning for purposes of wealth assessment, taxation, or trade or whatever other statistically-based exercise may have been involved. Even here there are reservations to be made, however. It is worth noting that although clay tokens used for such purposes could hardly retain any emblematic character *in that context*, nevertheless they still trail clouds of numerical glory. For is it not still magical that numbers transfer automatically and infallibly from the individual animals in the field to the pieces of clay on the accountant's shelf? To be sure, familiarity with magic breeds contempt for magic. But the fact that a thirsty priest corrupted by professional practice may take a swig from the bottle of holy communion wine does not *ipso facto* prove the wine to be mere booze. In that sense, whole professions may be corrupt. For all we know, accountancy in Mesopotamia may have been a corrupt profession.

The earliest writing implement? Three views of the 'Ishango bone'. Institut
Royal des Sciences Naturelles de Belgique, Brussels.

What is relevant for our present purposes is the fact that
counting is associated in many cultures with primitive forms of
recording which have a graphically isomorphic basis. This is
the use of marks taking the shape of simple linear notches or

strokes.[4] One notch or stroke is added to an inventory for every item to be counted, and the total, when required, is calculated by addition of the individual marks. The iconic origin of such recording systems is hardly open to doubt: the notch or stroke corresponds to the human finger. For finger-counting is a practice attested the world over. The advantage of this method of recording is that in effect it gives the record-keeper an unlimited number of graphic fingers to count on. Its flexibility, but also its limitation, resides in the fact that it does not record any information about the kinds of items being counted. The row of strokes, in other words, is a graphic equivalent to the gesture of holding up a certain number of fingers. The strokes no more tell us what is being counted than the fingers do. In short, the rows of strokes are graphically isomorphic with just that subpart of the recorder's oral language which comprises the corresponding words used for counting. It makes no difference whether we 'read' the sign pictorially as standing for so many fingers held up, or scriptorially as standing for a certain numeral.

The isomorphism, however, is of a structurally different variety from the isomorphism of emblematic symbols. The individual strokes in the row have no fixed correspondence to any particular numeral. We can add them up from left to right, or from right to left, or in any order we please – not necessarily in the order in which they were inscribed; provided always that each is counted just once. The matching condition for sign-systems of this kind is simply one-to-one token correspondence: while the perspicuity condition is that each token be denumerably individuated from all its fellows.

Evidently, mere rows of strokes will become inadequate as

---

[4] If the prehistoric bone tool from the Ishango site in Zaire was, as has been suggested, a writing instrument and the carvings on it a calendrical or numerical notation, evidence for the use of token-iterative signs in connexion with writing could date back to as early as 9000 B.C. (J. de Heinzelin, 'Ishango', *Scientific American*, Vol.206, No.6, June 1962, pp.105-114; C. Zaslavsky, *Africa Counts*, Boston, 1973, p.17ff.)

signs once it is desired to record information which cannot simply be 'recovered' from the visible marks by means of the subsequent counting operation. At this point it becomes necessary to have recourse to some semiological principle other than 'one mark = one countable item'. And that point is soon reached. As soon, in fact, as a situation arises in which items of two or more types are to be inventoried separately in the same record. It will be unsatisfactory in many circumstances to rely solely on memory in order to determine retrospectively which row of strokes stood for sheep and which row of strokes stood for goats. The problem is exactly analogous to that of having two piles of pebbles and not being able to remember which was the 'sheep' pile and which was the 'goat' pile. The problem becomes even more crucial if the person subsequently reckoning the marks is someone other than the person who originally made them. One solution to that communicational problem is to adopt different types of mark to distinguish between as many different types of item as need to be inventoried. It is here that the emblematic sign presents itself as an obvious candidate which might be pressed into service for just this purpose. For it has precisely those specific identificatory virtues which strokes and notches conspicuously lack.

The cultural prerequisites for taking such a step, however, are not to be underestimated. It presupposes, for example, breaking with any prior cultural taboo about the use of emblems; or else – and this might be potentially no less sacrilegious in certain civilisations – devising new emblems or quasi-emblematic signs to 'stand for' the range of animals or other types of item to be inventoried. The existence of such taboos could explain, in fact, the earliest adoption of 'arbitrary' symbols or tokens of the kind which seem to have been used in the Mesopotamian counting system. The employment of 'arbitrary' shapes for purposes of keeping records may well have been a primitive compromise between the significance of the emblem and the insignificance of the pebble. However, the use of the term 'arbitrary' in this connexion must be hedged about for obvious reasons with all kinds of qualifications. The fact is that we do not know what symbolic or emblematic values may have originally attached to shapes and configurations which to a modern eye appear to be simply 'geometric'.

Granted that, for whatever reason, the adaptation of emblematic or quasi-emblematic signs was culturally acceptable as a solution to the problem of distinguishing between different types of item to be recorded in the same inventory, it remains to observe that in principle there are two ways of implementing this possibility.

One solution is to have lists in which, for instance, the symbol representing a sheep is repeated once for every sheep counted. Likewise, the symbol representing a goat is repeated once for every goat counted. This system is equivalent to having an unlimited supply of toy sheep and toy goats, or similar clay animal figures. Simply by adding to or taking away from the store of different figures, an up-to-date record may be kept of the animal population. The graphic counterpart of the clay-figure inventory will be drawing one symbol of a sheep or a goat for every sheep or goat kept, and adding or erasing such symbols as necessary, in accordance with births, deaths, and market sales or barters, in order to keep the current tally.

A possibly less time-consuming solution, however, is to combine the principle of having separate symbols for representing sheep and goats with the principle of counting strokes. Thus instead of repeating the sheep-symbol four times over in order to record four sheep, the record would show one sheep-symbol followed by four strokes. (This would be equivalent to having one clay figure representing sheep, on which the Mesopotamian accountant marked one incision for every sheep in the flock.) And *mutatis mutandis* for goats.

The point to be noted here is that although both lists make the same information available, they involve using marks in different ways. In one list, a tally of four sheep will be recorded by setting down four identical sheep-symbols, one after another. In the other type of list, the same information will be recorded by means of one instance of the sheep-symbol, followed by four strokes. The difference is important as far as the structure of the sign-system is concerned. In the former case the sheep-symbol itself becomes the token to be counted; whereas in the latter case the sheep-symbol is simply a classificatory device, and only the accompanying strokes are counted in the reckoning. Clearly, other forms of token-iterative listing would be possible. It would be possible, for instance, to have lists in which the sheep-symbol followed by one stroke recorded two sheep: thus the sheep-symbol would function simultaneously as a type-indicator and also as a countable token in just one instance. If the recording system is to fulfil its purpose, in short, it becomes necessary to decide which of various possible listing conventions to adopt. Whichever is adopted, this will mean incorporating certain structurally superimposed features upon the system of signs employed. And this, in turn, is the thin end of the semiological wedge which will ultimately prise pictorial and scriptorial signs apart. For the combination of two primordially different signs in the same graphic system opens up communicational possibilities which were not inherent in either type of sign individually.

Whatever its magical overtones or implications, graphic isomorphism cannot survive a certain degree of elaboration. There are quite general semiological considerations which force us to this conclusion. To bring home the point, it will be useful to show how it applies to a situation in which graphic isomorphism is *ex hypothesi* present in a purely 'utilitarian' system of signs.

Let us consider a very simple communicational system of the kind described by Wittgenstein in the opening paragraphs of the *Philosophische Untersuchungen*.[5] The *dramatis personae* in

---

[5] L. Wittgenstein, *Philosophische Untersuchungen*, tr. G.E.M. Anscombe, 2nd. ed., Oxford, 1958, § 2ff.

Wittgenstein's example are a builder and his assistant. They are using four kinds of building materials: blocks, slabs, pillars and beams. Every time the builder needs one of these, he calls out the word for block, slab, pillar or beam, as the case may be, and his assistant fetches one. Those four words constitute the entire language. Clearly it would make no difference what the four words were, provided they were distinct: they might be *bloop, bleep, blip* and *blop*, for example. Nor would it change the example if there were more than four different types of building materials involved. There could be as many as we wish, provided the language has a separate word for each.

Let us now elaborate Wittgenstein's example. Suppose at times the noise of bulldozers on the building site is deafening, and the builder cannot make himself heard. So he draws a picture of a block, slab, pillar or beam, as the case may be, whenever he wants the assistant to fetch one. Better still, he has four cards showing a block, a slab, a pillar and a beam; and he holds up the appropriate card when the noise is too loud to shout the corresponding word. This card-system will serve us as a paradigm case of graphic isomorphism in the following sense: it is a matter of complete indifference to the efficiency of the communication system whether a card is 'read' scriptorially as the sign for a spoken word or pictorially as the sign for a type of object. For it will 'mean the same' in either case, as regards its function in the communication situation. Furthermore the card-system and the word-system implement exactly parallel matching and perspicuity conditions. Any sequence of cards shown will match a corresponding sequence of words uttered; and both pictures and words must be identifiably distinct from the contrasting pictures and words.

Now, finally, let us kick away the scaffolding involved in having elaborated Wittgenstein's original example. That will leave us with a communication system in which, *ab initio*, there is a graphic isomorphism of a purely utilitarian nature – even utilitarian in the sense that is 'easier' for the builder to utter the next verbal command while proceeding with the manual effort of building than to interrupt that process in order to hold up a card. Which strategy he employs on any given occasion will therefore depend simply on the prevailing noise-level: again, a utilitarian solution. Thus there is no primacy of the oral sign over the visual sign other than the primacy which flows from the advantage of being able to do two things at once. That primacy would automatically be eroded if the builder were an octopus and consequently found it much easier to hold a card aloft while putting slabs in place than to put slabs in place at the same time as generating enough muscular laryngeal effort to produce a noise identifiable as the vocable for 'slab'.

Next, we may examine what might happen if a further refinement of this system were required. Suppose at one stage in the building work it becomes necessary at times to distinguish between red blocks and blue blocks, red slabs and blue slabs, long beams and short beams, long pillars and short pillars. Orally, this new requirement is met by introducing four new words into the language: that is to say, words for 'red', 'blue', 'long' and 'short'. When the builder wants a red block he now has to utter two words, namely the word for 'red' followed by the word for 'block'. Similarly, when he wants a long beam he has to utter the word for 'long' followed by the word for 'beam'. Thus eight new two-word combinations enter the language, although the four original words are still available as single instructions when it does not matter for the builder's immediate purpose about the colour or the length of the object to be fetched.

Changes will also be required in the card-system if it is to fulfil these new communicational needs. Suppose four new cards are introduced. Two of these show simply colour samples: red and blue. The other two show a long line and a short line respectively. Under this new system the builder signals for a red block by holding up the red card and then the card showing the picture of a block; for a long beam, by holding up the card with the long line and then the card showing the picture of a beam; and likewise for the other card-combinations. But he can still hold up one of the original four cards by itself when he is not concerned to specify the colour or the length of the object he needs.

In this way, the card-system keeps in line with the word-system at all points. The inventory of signs and of sign-combinations remains in exact one-to-one correspondence. But what has happened is that the card-system has begun to lose its original iconic character. For although the card showing the black-and-white block-shape is still a picture of a block, that does not make a black-and-white shape followed by a separate red colour sample a picture of a red block; any more than a blank cheque and a signature on a separate piece of paper together constitute a signed cheque. In the case of the block-shape and the colour sample, there is no combined 'picture of a red block' because the physical separation of the significant elements of shape and colour destroys that synthesis which we recognise as an essential characteristic of visual experience and of pictures.

It would, however, be possible to introduce a different card-system in which that characteristic visual synthesis was preserved. This could be done by designing eight new picture-cards, including some coloured ones. One of these would show a red block, another a blue block, another a red slab, and another a blue slab. The other four new cards would show a long beam, a short beam, a long pillar and a short pillar. These eight new cards would supplement the original four, making twelve in all. This would meet all the communicational requirements of the new situation in the building operation, and retain the iconically synthetic character of the signs. But now there would no longer under this twelve-card system be the same one-to-one correspondence between cards and words. There would be no single card corresponding to the word for 'red', for example.

The builder, in short, here faces a forced choice. Either he can preserve the one-to-one correspondence between elements of the visual system and elements of the oral system; or else he can preserve the original iconic character of the cards. But he cannot achieve both simultaneously. Whichever option is chosen, the complete graphic isomorphism of the original card system can no longer be maintained. If he opts for preserving the iconic character of the cards by adopting the twelve-card system, then although each individual card can still be 'read' not only as a sign of a type of object but also as a sign of a particular word or word-combination, nevertheless there is no single card which can be 'read' as representing the word 'blue' or the word 'long'; nor is there any sequence of cards which can be 'read' as the word-sequence 'long beam'. Alternatively, if he opts for preserving a one-to-one correspondence with the oral language by choosing the eight-card system, there will be no single card which can be 'read' as a picture of a red block, or as a picture of a long beam.

What this illustrates is how, given an original system of graphically isomorphic signs, its adaptation to more complex communicational requirements will lead to the intrusion of structurally superimposed features which inevitably open up a gap of just the kind which characteristically separates pictures from writing.

Returning now to the no less remote ambiance of prehistoric Mesopotamian accountancy and its choice of possible listing principles, one point emerges clearly enough. All the token-iterative systems previously described have the same disadvantage. They leave the record-keeper to do the counting every time an assessment of totals is required. In the case of four sheep, the problem is negligible. In the case of sixty sheep, it looms larger. In the case of four thousand sheep it begins to assume formidable proportions. Had there been no graphic solution available to this recording problem, civilisation would almost certainly have remained at a very primitive level (as judged by the educational and technological standards of the modern world) and writing as we now know it would probably never have emerged at all.

The 'great invention' was almost certainly the prehistoric move from a token-iterative to an 'emblem-slotting' system for recording numerical information. Whereas token-iterative systems can just as easily be used in the form of sets of clay counters or beads on strings as in the form of graphic signs, graphic signs have the great advantage of being more easily adaptable to recording systems based on an emblem-slotting semiology.

The essential difference between iterative listing and slot-listing is that the latter requires separate symbols for individual integers. A slot list comprises, as a minimum, just two signs. One of the two signs fills the 'slot' reserved for indicating the type of item inventoried, while the other fills the complementary 'slot' reserved for indicating the total. The progression from recording sixty sheep by means of one 'sheep' sign followed by sixty strokes to recording the same information by means of one 'sheep' sign followed by a second sign indicating 'sixty' is a progression which has already crossed the boundary between pictorial and scriptorial signs. A token-iterative sign-system is in effect equivalent to a verbal sublanguage which is restricted to messages of the form 'sheep, sheep, sheep, sheep ... ', or 'sheep, another, another, another ...'; whereas an emblem-slotting system is equivalent to a sublanguage which can handle messages of the form 'sheep, sixty'. Token-iterative lists are, in principle, lists as long as the number of individual items recorded. With a slot list, on the other hand, we get no information simply by counting the number of marks it contains.

Slotting is a structural technique we now regard as intrinsic to language; and nowhere more typically than in the way languages deal with counting. The languages of all mathematically sophisticated civilisations assign separate words to integers, and characteristically designate the number of items in any given set by combining one or more of the language's 'number-words' with another word designating the class of items in question (*sixty sheep, soixante moutons*, etc.).

The crucial point here is that slotting is a semiological principle intrinsic to oral language the world over, not merely in respect of the vocabulary of counting, but in respect of all other areas of vocabulary as well. Slotting imposes an analytic structure of its own on the way signs are used for purposes of communication, irrespective of the specific message involved. Thus the key difference between, say, a row of identical animal-signs and one animal-sign followed by a single number-sign is in an important respect parallel to the difference between the builder's twelve-card system, which indicates a red block by means of a single picture of a red block, and the eight-card system, which conveys the same message by means of one card showing the outline of a block, together with another card showing a red colour sample. The eight-card system, unlike the twelve-card system, is a system which uses the slotting principle. It is typical of linguistic structure, as opposed to pictorial representation, to 'separate' properties and quantities from objects, and express them by means of independent signs.

Although the example discussed above relates to a specially prominent social need, namely the keeping of accurate accounts, the postulated principle of scriptorial development itself has nothing to do with counting as such. It could equally well be illustrated, for instance, from the development of a musical notation. As it happens, even the earliest surviving systems of musical notation we know are either based on or contaminated by pre-existing forms of writing of a more general nature (as exemplified in the familiar adoption of the names of letters of the alphabet to designate musical notes: A,B,C,D,E ...).[6] But it is by no means out of the question that there might once have been more 'primitive' forms of musical notation which were independent of such ties. Nor is it difficult to see how such notations might have begun with an

---

[6] *The New Grove Dictionary of Music and Musicians*, London, 1980, Vol.13, 'Notation'.

original graphic isomorphism.

One might envisage, for example, the following way of recording tunes to be played on a primitive type of flute or pipe. Each note is indicated by means of a drawing showing the instrument in an upright position, mouthpiece at the top, with the holes pierced in the tubular body, and a finger covering each hole to be blocked when playing the note in question. A sequence of notes would be indicated by a series of such drawings. It is significant that drawings of essentially this character are nowadays to be found only in very elementary instruction manuals for beginners. Such signs may be regarded as being in graphically isomorphic correspondence with a certain set of musical notes. A sign system of this kind clearly already takes very many things for granted. It takes for granted that the apprentice musician realises that notes are produced by exhaling into the mouthpiece of the instrument, that the note produced will correspond to the configuration of 'open' and 'blocked' holes, and so on. All these assumptions constitute what might collectively be called the 'pragmatic preconditions' for having any graphic recording system for playing the instrument at all.

Nor is it difficult to see the steps by which an original system of this kind might be simplified, for reasons of convenience and economy. If the apprentice musicians already know how many holes the instrument has, and which holes are most conveniently covered by which fingers, then there is nothing to prevent a reduced schematisation of the 'full' pictorial details. The body of the upright flute can now be shown simply as a vertical bar, and the positions of the holes to be blocked can be shown by marking horizontal strokes at the appropriate positions along it. This immediately opens the way to representing each note in a sequence by an angular 'runic' character (of just the kind exemplified by our familiar capital letters 'T', 'E', 'F', and 'L'). In fact, a subset of alphabetic capitals provides in principle an adequately supplementable notation for recording tunes played on a pipe with just three holes. All it lacks are characters corresponding to the note played by blocking just the middle hole; to the note played by blocking the two lower holes; and to the note played by leaving just the middle hole open but blocking the other two (⊢, ⊨ and ⊏).

All this, however, rests on the musical premiss that one of these flute tunes is distinguished from another simply by its sequential characteristics as a set of notes of different pitch (with the underlying pragmatic precondition that the flute or pipe is so constructed that to each such note there corresponds one and only one fingering, granted that 'fingering' is construed simply in terms of blocking certain holes and leaving others open). The situation changes radically once 'tunes' are no longer communicationally identifiable simply in terms of pitch sequences. As soon as quantitative information is also required – that is, as soon as musicians count the duration and volume of a note as features no less important than its pitch – this creates problems of a very basic nature for the graphic recording system. These problems are exactly parallel to those confronting Wittgenstein's builder as soon as it becomes communicationally necessary to distinguish between the colours and the dimensions of the building materials in question. There is a forced choice between endeavouring to maintain an original graphic isomorphism, and sacrificing this isomorphism to a new principle of representation which allows the various features of the note to be shown by separate graphic signs, occupying separate slots in a sign-combination. The moment we choose to show the difference between a long note and a short note of the same pitch by marking the former by means of a 'tail' or a superscript 'bar', and the latter by absence of any such mark, then we have crossed the divide between pictorial and scriptorial signs. A picture of a long note is not a drawing of the blocked holes, plus a separate length mark; any more than a picture of a red block is a drawing of a block, plus a separate colour sample.

*

A quite general mechanism underlying the development of scriptorial signs may thus be described in the following terms: the need to record more complex information, or to record it in a more convenient form, may introduce superimposed structural features which disrupt an original graphic isomorphism in various ways. It is in this context that the frequency with which we encounter the rebus as a device used in early writing systems assumes its full significance. The rebus represents an attempt to cling to the principle of graphic isomorphism as an 'ideal' form of representation. In other words, it seeks to provide pictorial signs for recording information which cannot otherwise be represented pictorially at all, because it is information which is essentially non-visual.

Recent Heineken advertisement: the rebus refreshes the parts alphabetic advertising cannot reach.

If, for example, a writing system has a pictogram which takes the form of a four-winged insect, to be read either as the noun *bee* or as the verb *be*, depending on context, what that shows is that at some earlier stage the verb was felt to present a problem for the graphic system precisely *because* it had no obvious pictorial counterpart. Instead of just inventing an arbitrary graphic sign to be read as the verb *be*, a better solution was felt to consist in 'borrowing' the graphically isomorphic insect-sign of the fortuitously homophonous noun *bee*. This type of borrowing does not constitute an attempt to write phonetically at all. On the contrary, it is a bold attempt to bring an awkward case into line with a preferred form of scripto-pictorial parallelism.

Three important points concerning language must be noted in connexion with this general mechanism underlying the evolution of scriptorial signs. First, the mechanism itself does not lead automatically or ineluctably in the direction of the kind of writing system on which Western education came to be based. It is just as capable of leading in the opposite direction to the development of graphic systems which are independent of oral communication altogether. A musical notation, for instance, does not need the backing of a musical metalanguage if the musicians can 'read' its signs directly in terms of fingering techniques, strategies of breath control, and other playing skills which can in principle be learned directly by imitation from a teacher rather than by oral explanation. The extent to which a musical notation may become 'international' is striking proof of the fact that we are here dealing with a mode of communication which, in the final analysis, has no linguistic basis at all. But that does not make musical notation any the less a form of writing. Nor would it be any the less so if the notes, fingering positions, etc. had no verbal names in any known language. That would not prove whether or not musical notation had an emblematic point of departure. We do not know. Perhaps it did. Perhaps music is more ancient than counting. The flute-holes may conceivably have been construed as primitive emblems of the moon, because flute-players were priests of the moon goddess. That is not what is at issue here.

A second point is that the development of graphic signs which are in essence independent of verbal communication is often masked by the ease with which such signs may, if necessary, be supplied with an appropriate verbal terminology for purposes of discussion. The development of mathematical notation provides an obvious example. It puts the cart before the horse to think of the sign $\sqrt{}$ as a symbolic substitute or abbreviation for the words 'square root of'. On the contrary, the sign indicates a mathematical operation which does not in any way depend on having verbal terms to designate it (and which in any case can only doubtfully be defined in the vocabulary of ordinary language without tying that vocabulary into verbal knots). More generally, mathematics offers a paradigm case of conceptual development which would be 'unthinkable' without the availability of a graphic notation in which to 'do the thinking' involved. For graphic signs offer advantages of symbol manipulation for which other forms of symbolism, including speech, offer only clumsy alternatives (if indeed they offer any alternatives at all). It suffices to think about the problem of representing the square root of minus one on an abacus to convince oneself that for certain purposes there is no substitute for writing. But once the exploitation of a certain graphic system has led to new conceptual developments, it is no major problem to supply any associated verbal system with a new vocabulary to deal with it. This conclusion is already implicit in the elaborated fable of Wittgenstein's building site. The builder will always have the choice either of bringing the card-system into line with the oral language, or vice versa, whatever new information about building materials becomes essential to the operation. Sometimes he may choose the former option, sometimes the latter. This will not necessarily be detrimental to communicational efficiency. All kinds of hybrid solutions to any such communicational problems are possible.

The third point is that if we take this general mechanism as a plausible basis for explaining the evolution of scriptorial signs, it becomes clear that to treat the representation of speech as criterial for recognising the emergence of writing is to fall victim to a fallacy of historical retrospection not just once but twice over. On the one hand, there is no basis for distinguishing the pictorial from the scriptorial function of graphic signs until we already at least conceive of the possibility of signs which are non-isomorphic. On the other hand, it is circular to force a 'Bayeux tapestry' interpretation on examples from civilisations which we cannot assume to have been aware of anything like our own distinction between the pictorial and the scriptorial. For instance, it is question-begging to treat the pre-Conquest Mixtec codices of Central America as examples of a graphic system which somehow 'got stuck'; that is, started on the evolution towards writing, but never quite achieved it. That interpretation is based on picking out certain Mixtec graphic conventions and equating them with what we now call writing *as opposed to* drawing or painting; and, correlatively, treating other Mixtec graphic conventions as 'merely pictorial'. Thus, for instance, the use of the symbol which shows an arrow penetrating a place-sign is said to be logographic, on the ground that the symbol stands for conquest and one of the idioms for this notion in spoken Mixtec was, literally translated, 'to put an arrow in the lands of another'. By contrast, however, the symbolisation of marriage by showing a male and a female sharing the same platform, or the indication of parenthood by showing an umbilical cord linking one figure to another, are dismissed as 'strictly pictorial' conventions.[7] This distinction is all the more bizarre inasmuch as it is generally recognised that the histories which these codices set down were meant to

[7] M.E. Smith, *Picture Writing from Ancient Southern Mexico*, Norman, Oklahoma, 1973, p.174.

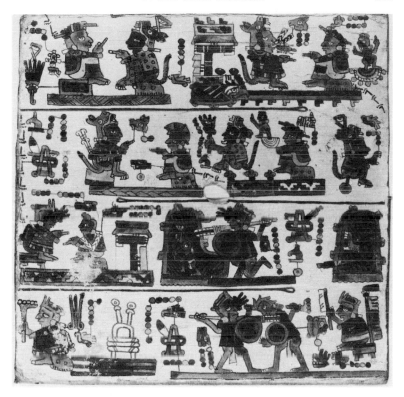

Mixtec symbolisation of the marriage relationship: a seated man and woman facing each other on a low platform. Bodleian Library ms Arch. Seld. A,2, sheet 13.

be read' by priests or other officials specially trained in this particular form of recording.[8] In other words, there is no parallel at all with the case of the naive Western student who claims to be able to 'read the pictures' of the Bayeux tapestry because they 'speak to the eye', but not to be able to read the accompanying text because he knows no Latin.

To put it more generally, what we count as 'reading' must inevitably be relative to particular cultural purposes, and

[8] ibid., p.20. A.R. Pagden, *Mexican Pictorial Manuscripts*, Oxford, 1972, p.3.

depend on the contrasting modes of oral rendition which a particular culture may have institutionalised. It is a gross *non sequitur* to conclude that the Mixtec codices are only in part 'written' texts on the ground that the typical oral performance with which they were associated would have left much scope for individual variation in 'reading' as between one performer and another. That would be like questioning the status of musical notation on the ground that two musicians might play the same score differently. Both examples assume criteria of standardisation and homogeneity which are brought in like *dei ex machina* to solve a conceptual problem. What the Mixtec example illustrates is the modern difficulty of thinking about graphic systems at all without tacitly erecting our own standards of expectation concerning the correspondence between the written and the spoken word into cultural panchronic universals.

It is not simply that we have no means of knowing whether Mixtec civilisation in the pre-Conquest era had any distinction matching our distinction between 'reading what the text says' and 'telling what the pictures show'; but rather that the very concept of oral rendition is itself dependent upon the graphic system or systems which provide its basis. From our modern vantage-point, we find it quite easy to see that because the spelling of the English word *bath* does not indicate whether a speaker should pronounce it with a back vowel or a front vowel it would be absurd to insist that this is a word which cannot be read aloud at all. At the same time, we find it remarkably difficult to concede that by the same token it may be no less absurd to insist that a Mixtec priest giving an oral rendition of the codices was not reading them, on the ground that the text in front of him did not consistently indicate exactly which Mixtec sentences to utter. We have no licence to assume that 'sentences', unlike 'pronunciations', are units which enjoy a special culture-neutral status, enabling them to be identified without reference to any associated graphic system. On the contrary, the history of Western linguistics suggests that without reference to an established graphic tradition, it may be extremely difficult for the mind to grasp general criteria of oral 'sameness' which would ground any conceptualisation of linguistic units at all.

There is a world of difference between saying that certain forms of writing adapt verbal models to provide solutions to various problems of graphic communication, and saying that writing exists solely and simply to set down what people say. The latter claim is straightforwardly false, and it does modern linguistics no credit to have erected that falsehood into a theoretical dogma. Oral communication is certainly not the only source of structural analogues which contributed to systematising a distinction between pictorial and scriptorial forms of graphic expression (even if, from certain points of view, it may be regarded as the most important source). The idea of genius behind the great invention of writing was an intuitive grasp of the principle that graphic signs have no limitations for purposes of human communication other than those which derive causally from their primary parameters as visible marks. *They have no other semiological constraints.* In short, the idea of genius was the idea of graphic communication as a mode of communication *sui generis.* Its pivotal implementation was no doubt the practical move from token-iterative signs to type-slotting signs as a way of recording numerical information.

To see that graphic communication is a mode of communication *sui generis* is to see that graphic signs are free to be adapted – systematically or unsystematically – to any particular communicational purpose desired. It is to see that they can be used to 'draw' the configuration of someone's name, or of a musical note, or of a number, or of a day of the week, just as well as to 'draw' the outline of an animal or the shape of a pot. It is also to see, at the same time, that the resources of graphic signs as such go far beyond any one particular cultural practice or function with which they may have been associated. It thus involves seeing, for example, that the communicational potential of graphic marks is not restricted by some special inalienable and untransferable relationship binding particular marks emblematically to particular creatures and their names; any more than by particular roles played in some procedure laid down for keeping accounts or performing religious ceremonies.

In the hindsight of history, that primary idea of genius tends to be eclipsed by another idea of equal genius. This was the realisation that therefore graphic communication, as a mode of communication *sui generis*, is free to draw upon other modes of communication as structural models. In particular, it could draw upon oral communication as an incomparably rich source of analogies for the graphic expression of all kinds of information that human beings might need for purposes of civilisation. That is what eventually set writing on the royal road to the alphabet. If we are to give full credit to the originality of these initial perceptions, it is important not to lose sight of the fact that what scripts have in common with musical and mathematical notations is a recognition that invented systems of graphic signs do not need to be tied to visual interpretations, even though every individual sign has to be visually identifiable. That means, in brief, that one is free to introduce, for communicational purposes, patterns of structuring which can be interpreted by reference to experience of any relevant kind whatsoever, or to none. Visual experience is simply one of the possible sources: the experience of oral communication is another. What we now call 'painting', 'drawing' and related forms of graphic 'art' are simply those forms of graphic communication which have retained iconicity as a basis for the elaboration of graphic conventions; whereas what we now call 'writing' are those forms of graphic communication which have, in different ways, sought to exploit various alternatives. It is in this sense that writing stands at the basis of the picture just as much as the picture stands at the basis of writing.

Doubtless the human race has not so far exploited anything

like the full range of communicational possibilities made available by this twin recognition of the independence of graphic signs and their structural plasticity. It took, obviously enough, a conceptual revolution in prehistoric times to realise that graphic signs can show what is invisible as clearly and as fully as they can show what is visible; that they can capture certain structures of aural or manipulative or kinetic experience just as definitely as certain structures of visual experience. But the merely technical transition to recording by means of marks on a more-or-less flat surface had, *per se*, nothing to do with it. Obviously, there is no great conceptual advance involved in scratching stones or impressing clay. What may be less obvious is the inevitability of the fact that every change in perspective from which the independence of writing is viewed brings with it an automatic re-evaluation of the boundary between the pictorial and the non-pictorial, together with a re-evaluation of the relationship between speech and language. This must be true not only for all past but for all future developments in human communication. The independence of the scriptorial sign is now such as to guarantee our descendants' re-evaluations in advance, irrespective of whether or not they still call their preferred forms of electronic literacy 'writing'. From their point of view, needless to say, the 'origin of writing' may well turn out to be a point in the history of human sign-systems which we ourselves, in the late twentieth century, have not yet reached. And, like us, they may continue to use the ancestral forms of writing without recognising them for what they are.

Epilogue

It says a great deal about Western culture that the question of the origin of writing could be posed clearly for the first time only after the traditional dogmas about the relationship between speech and writing had been subjected both to the brash counterpropaganda of a McLuhan and to the inquisitorial scepticism of a Derrida. But it says even more that the question could not be posed clearly until writing itself had dwindled to microchip dimensions. Only with this latest of the communications revolutions did it become obvious that the origin of writing must be linked to the future of writing in ways which bypass speech altogether.

As intellectual labour, it would be toil in vain to re-plough McLuhan's field, or Derrida's either. They are ready for sowing, and the harvest will surely include in the fulness of time a history of writing *as writing*. When that history comes to be written – as distinct from the premature sketch we might now attempt – speech will be seen as the historical crutch on which writing was obliged to lean in the earliest phases, a prop to be thrown aside when no longer needed.

That history will also show us how Saussure was wrong to relegate writing to the status of an ancillary system merely designed to represent speech, but right to insist that speech was just one of many possible manifestations of a higher human faculty – that semiological faculty governing the creation of signs, which is '*la faculté linguistique par excellence*'.

Bibliography

Comparatively little has been written about the problem of the origin of writing, as distinct from the subsequent history of writing and of particular scripts, where the list of publications is endless. The standard surveys of the field in English (which still give the 'traditional' account of the origin of writing) are:

D. Diringer, *Writing*, London, 1962.
I.J. Gelb, *A Study of Writing*, 2nd ed., Chicago, 1963.

A more up-to-date presentation, which takes the modern concept of information storage as its starting point, is to be found in:

A. Gaur, *A History of Writing*, London, 1984.

All three have useful bibliographies; and Diringer and Gaur are copiously illustrated.

Ancient authorities on the question of the origin of writing include:

Diodorus Siculus, *Library of History*, III, 4, tr. C.H. Oldfather, London, 1935.
Herodotus, *History*, II, 2, tr. A.D. Godley, London, 1925.

The most extensive discussion of Egyptian writing, commonly assumed in antiquity to be the oldest form, is:

Horapollo, *Hieroglyphics*, tr. A.T. Cory, London, 1840.

A remarkable attempt to argue that the origin of writing preceded the origin of speech is to be found in:

J. van Ginneken, 'Die Bilderschrift-Sprachen', *Travaux du Cercle Linguistique de Prague*, Vol. 8, 1939; and 'La reconstruction typologique des langues archaïques de l'humanité', *Verhandelingen der K. Netherlandsche Akademie van Wetenschappen*, Letterkunde, N.R. xliv, Amsterdam, 1940.

On the origin and history of the alphabet, nothing has yet superseded:

D. Diringer, *The Alphabet*, 3rd ed., London, 1968.

The lavish volume of plates constitutes the fullest pictorial record of the history of writing so far published.

The most impressive case for linking the origin of writing to signs used in primitive systems of accounting is:

D. Schmandt-Besserat, 'The earliest precursor of writing', *Scientific American*, Vol.238, No.6, June 1978.

Also worth consulting in this connexion are:

A. Marshack, *The Roots of Civilization. The Cognitive Beginnings of Man's First Art, Symbol and Notation*, New York, 1972.
C. Zaslavsky, *Africa Counts*, Boston, 1973.

For criticism of Schmandt-Besserat's thesis, see:

I.J. Gelb, 'Principles of writing systems within the frame of visual communication', in P.A. Kolers, M.E. Wrolstad & H. Bouma (eds.), *Processing of Visible Language* 2, New York, 1980.

The old question of whether Franco-Cantabrian engraved signs of the Paleolithic period are not a form of writing is raised again in:

A. Forbes Jr. & T.R. Crowder, 'The problem of Franco-Cantabrian abstract signs: agenda for a new approach', *World Archeology*, Vol.10, 1979.

A readable introduction to modern attempts to decode early systems of writing is:

M. Pope, *The Story of Decipherment*, London, 1975.

On the modern controversy over the relationship between writing and speech, and the doctrine of the 'primacy of speech', see:

J. Derrida, *Of Grammatology*, tr. G.C. Spivak, Baltimore, 1976.

R. Harris, *The Language-Makers*, London, 1980, Ch.1.

F. Householder, *Linguistic Speculations*, Cambridge, 1971, Ch.13.

J. Lyons, 'Human language', in R.A. Hinde (ed.) *Non-Verbal communication*, Cambridge, 1972.

J. Vachek, *Written Language*, The Hague, 1973.

The impact of writing on culture has been extensively discussed, *inter alia* in:

J. Goody (ed.), *Literacy in Traditional Societies*, Cambridge, 1968.

E.A. Havelock, *Origins of Western Literacy*, Toronto, 1976; and *The Literate Revolution in Ancient Greece and its Cultural Consequences*, Princeton, 1982.

R. Hoggart, *The Uses of Literacy*, London, 1957.

M. McLuhan, *The Gutenberg Galaxy*, Toronto, 1962.

W.J. Ong, *Orality and Literacy*, London, 1982.
J.W. Thompson, *The Literacy of the Laity in the Middle Ages*, New York, 1963.

A well documented bibliography covering this field is:

H.J. Graff, *Literacy in History*, Chicago, 1976 (Supplement 1979).

For modern linguistic and psycholinguistic approaches to the analysis of writing systems, see various papers published in:

J.F. Kavanagh & I.G. Mattingly (eds.), *Language by Ear and by Eye*, Cambridge, Mass., 1972.

especially:

E.S. Klima, 'How alphabets might reflect language'.
S.E. Martin, 'Nonalphabetic writing systems'.
J. Lotz, 'How language is conveyed by script'.

See also:

P.T. Smith and H.M. Pattison, 'English shorthand systems and abbreviatory conventions: a psychological perspective', in P.A. Kolers, M.E. Wrolstad & H. Bouma (eds.), *Processing of Visible Language* 2, New York, 1980.

Various anthropological perspectives on writing are represented in:

F.L.K. Hsu, *The Study of Literate Civilizations*, New York, 1969.
G. Mallery, *Picture-Writing of the American Indians*, Washington, 1893.
M. Cohen et al., *L'écriture et la psychologie des peuples*, Paris, 1963.

Y.H. Safadi, *Islamic Calligraphy*, London, 1978.

Problems in devising writing systems for a variety of language are disussed in:

J.A. Fishman (ed.), *Advances in the Creation and Revision of Writing Systems*, The Hague, 1977.

For the origin and development of musical notation, one may usefully begin by consulting:

I.D. Bent, D. Hiley, M. Bent & G. Chew, 'Notation', *The New Grove Dictionary of Music and Musicians*, Vol.13, London, 1980.

Similarly, for the origin and development of dance notation:

A.H. Guest, 'Choreography and dance notation', *Encyclopaedia Britannica*, 15th ed., Chicago, 1977, Macropaedia Vol.4.

On writing materials and techniques, a useful introduction is:

A. Gaur, 'The process of writing', in *A History of Writing*, London, 1984, pp.35-58.

On writing from a semiological point of view, there is unfortunately no general bibliographical *vade mecum*.

Index